First Workshop on NLP Applications to Field Linguistics (Field Matters 2022)

Held at COLING 2022

Gyeongju, South Korea
16 October 2022

ISBN: 978-1-7138-6151-5

Printed from e-media with permission by:

Curran Associates, Inc.
57 Morehouse Lane
Red Hook, NY 12571

Some format issues inherent in the e-media version may also appear in this print version.

Printed with permission by Curran Associates, Inc. (2023)

Association for Computational Linguistics
209 N. Eighth Street
Stroudsburg, Pennsylvania 18360

Phone: 1-570-476-8006
Fax: 1-570-476-0860

acl@aclweb.org

Additional copies of this publication are available from:

Curran Associates, Inc.
57 Morehouse Lane
Red Hook, NY 12571 USA
Phone: 845-758-0400
Fax: 845-758-2633
Email: curran@proceedings.com
Web: www.proceedings.com

COLING

International Conference on Computational Linguistics

Proceedings of the Conference and Workshops

Message from the Program Chairs

Field Matters is a workshop focused on various applications of NLP methods to field linguistics and analysis of field data with the help of computational linguistics. On the one hand, field linguists document language data, but the fieldwork involves tons of manual annotation or analysis, which might be significantly sped up with computational instruments. On the other hand, NLP research brought methods for different tasks that show significant performance in high-resource languages, allowing to automate various routine tasks. The future development of NLP methods could gain from the language diversity of under-resourced languages.

Field Matters is aimed to combine linguistic fieldwork and NLP methods. Our workshop is hosted by the 29th International Conference on Computational Linguistics (COLING 2022). To provide the comprehensive diverse expertise in a multidisciplinary setting, we invited linguists and NLP researchers worldwide to our program committee. After the hard process of reviewing all submissions, the program committee chose nine papers for a poster or oral presentation at the workshop. Accepted papers illustrate the main idea of our workshop: how field linguistics may benefit from using contemporary methods of computational analysis and how the NLP community may evolve its methods with the help of under-resourced languages.

We are incredibly grateful to the Field Matters program committee, who worked on peer review to give meaningful comments for each submission and made this workshop possible. We want to thank the invited speakers, Antonios Anastasopoulos and Steven Bird, for contributing to the program. We would also like to mention all the authors who submitted their papers to our workshop, and we hope to continue to serve as a link between NLP specialists and field linguists.

You can find more details about the workshop on our website: https://field-matters.github.io/

Organising Committee

Program Chairs

Oleg Serikov, HSE University, AIRI, MIPT, RAS Linguistics
Ekaterina Voloshina, HSE University, AIRI
Anna Postnikova, HSE University
Elena Klyachko, Institute of Linguistics RAS, HSE University
Ekaterina Neminova, HSE University
Ekaterina Vylomova, University of Melbourne
Tatiana Shavrina, AIRI, SberDevices
Valentin Malykh, Huawei
Francis Tyers, Indiana University, HSE University
Timofey Arkhangelskiy, University of Hamburg
Vladislav Mikhailov, SberDevices, HSE University
Alena Fenogenova, SberDevices

Program Committee

Program Committee

Alexandre Arkhipov, University of Hamburg
Rolando Coto Solano, Dartmouth College
Emily Prud'hommeaux, Boston College
Robbie Jimmerson, Rochester Institute of Technology
Zoe Liu, Boston College
Harald Hammarström, Max Planck Institute for the Science of Human History
David R. Mortensen, Carnegie Mellon University
Saliha Muradoglu, The Australian National University (ANU)
Éric Le Ferrand, Charles Darwin University, Université Grenoble Alpes
He Zhou (Indiana University Bloomington)
Ezequiel Koile, HSE University, Max Planck Institute for the Science of Human History
Bonaventure Dossou, Jacobs University Bremen
Chris C. Emezue, Technical University Munich
William Lane, Charles Darwin University
John Mansfield, University of Melbourne
Vitaly Protasov, AIR Institute
Svetlana Toldova, HSE University
Daan van Esch, Google Research
Oleg Serikov, HSE University, AIRI, MIPT, RAS Linguistics
Ekaterina Voloshina, HSE University, AIRI
Elena Klyachko, Institute of Linguistics RAS, HSE University
Ekaterina Vylomova, University of Melbourne
Tatiana Shavrina, AIRI, SberDevices
Valentin Malykh, Huawei
Timofey Arkhangelskiy, University of Hamburg
Vladislav Mikhailov, SberDevices, HSE University
George Moroz, HSE University
Daniil Ignatiev, HSE University

Invited Speakers

Antonios Anastasopoulos, George Mason University
Steven Bird, Charles Darwin University

Table of Contents

A Finite State Approach to Interactive Transcription

William Lane and Steven Bird
Northern Institute
Charles Darwin University

Abstract

We describe a novel approach to transcribing morphologically complex, local, oral languages. The approach connects with local motivations for participating in language work which center on language learning, accessing the content of audio collections, and applying this knowledge in language revitalization and maintenance. We develop a constraint-based approach to interactive word completion, expressed using Optimality Theoretic constraints, implemented in a finite state transducer, and applied to an Indigenous language. We show that this approach suggests correct full word predictions on 57.9% of the test utterances, and correct partial word predictions on 67.5% of the test utterances. In total, 87% of the test utterances receive full or partial word suggestions which serve to guide the interactive transcription process.

1 Introduction

Thousands of the world's languages have small populations and are characterized by primary oral usage (Ong, 1982). These local languages co-exist alongside trade languages, i.e., languages of commerce, education, mass media, and government. Local languages are generally losing ground to larger languages, a process known as language shift (Fishman, 2001). Key features of local languages are that they generally have no literary tradition, and little incentive exists for writing. There is often no established or widely known orthography, and usually no widely accepted standard variety to render into writing. The point where a related dialect becomes a distinct language may not be clearly understood or widely agreed.

Many heritage communities seek to reclaim or revitalize their ancestral languages (Hinton and Hale, 2001; Grenoble and Whaley, 2006). Here, people often depend on historical sources, including informal collections of audio recordings, in order to access the ancestral code. Scholars are also involved, using historical recordings in the process of language documentation and description (Woodbury, 2003). Ideally, everything would be transcribed, and it would be easy to access the content of such collections for the purposes of learning and scholarship. However, given that these are oral languages, there is usually no pool of readily available transcribers to call upon.

None of the above is systematically addressed by current low-resource approaches to transcription, which require upwards of 100k words (or 12-27 hours) of training data in the language, in order for sufficiently accurate phone recognition to support reasonable word error rates. Such work generally assumes that a comprehensive lexicon is available, and we find that this is generally not the case.

We seek a new approach, one that works with the locally available resources and human capacities. Our work is founded on three insights. First, work on Indigenous languages proceeds from locally meaningful, locally motivated activities. This usually prioritizes content over form, interpreting over transcribing (Bouquiaux and Thomas, 1992; Wilkins, 2000). Two important use cases are language learning and accessing the content of media collections. We devise tasks that leverage informal linguistic knowledge, such as the ability to form morphotactically valid words, and specialized knowledge of the vocabulary that pertains to a semantic domain of interest. This insight does not simply connect with local motivation, it is an effective way to meet the reciprocity requirement for ethical Indigenous research (NHMRC, 2018).

Second, work with speakers of Indigenous languages is more effective when it involves collaboration on realistic tasks. Thus, we operate within the skill set and time availability of speakers and linguists. In particular, we eschew artificial tasks like phonetic transcription, instead tapping into people's ability to identify words in connected speech (Meakins et al. 2018, 230; Bird 2020). This can in-

Proceedings of the first workshop on NLP applications to field linguistics, pages 1–10
July 5–10, 2020.
https://doi.org/10.26615/978-954-452-056-4_001

volve learning vocabulary, and getting clear about nuances of word meaning by drawing on usage in context, or speech concordances. Third, we apply what is known about the language, even when it is a non machine readable grammar, by interpreting it into a computational form that can be deployed to guide language tasks.

Thus, our contribution is a novel approach to transcribing local languages that is: locally motivated, feasible, and leverages what is already known about the language. As proof of concept we provide a finite state implementation, using the framework of constraint-based Optimality Theory (Prince and Smolensky, 2004; Ellison, 1994). We envisage that this implementation, suitably optimized, could be deployed in an interactive, collaborative, sparse transcription system.

2 Background

2.1 Sparse Transcription

The initial phase of working with a language – prior to having 100k words of transcribed audio – is characterized by uncertainty (Newman and Ratliff, 2001; Crowley, 2007). We have elicited enough words to establish the phonemic inventory, and transition to working with texts (Hale, 2001). However, when we listen to connected speech, we are only able to identify a few familiar words; the rest is a sea of undifferentiated speech sounds. We may attempt a transcription of those sounds, but the presence of coarticulation and disfluencies confounds our efforts to segment them and produce a contiguous transcription.

A popular solution is for linguists to delegate transcription work to literate speakers (King, 2015). However, as we have noted, for many oral languages it can be difficult to find suitable people. Instead, we may ask someone to carefully "re-speak" a recording, phrase by phrase (Woodbury, 2003, 11). Here we have found, for every place where we have conducted fieldwork, that speakers find this task immensely tedious. A solution is offered by *collaborative transcription*, where non-linguist speakers and non-speaker linguists work together.

Collaborative transcription, as we have experienced it, involves a speaker and a linguist listening to a recording, while revising a partial transcription consisting of words that the linguist has identified in connected speech. Between the identified words is unidentified material, hence the term "sparse transcription" (Bird, 2020). We illustrate this in (1), showing four iterations of linguist guesses and speaker confirmations. Not shown here is the fact that, between each iteration, we consider dozens of other utterances containing the words, and detect new, frequent words to add to our lexicon. Steps (a) and (d) may be separated in time by several days, a period during which the linguist is steadily learning to recognize a larger set of words in connected speech.

(1)

In (1), the x's indicate mismatches between phone recognizer output and the canonical transcriptions of the lexicon. These are leveraged in the optimality theoretic approach we set out below.

Sparse transcription is a shift away from current practices of transcribing phones, transcribing first, and transcribing fully (Bird, 2020). Instead, the focus is on local capacity and aspirations, and how these feed into and draw from semi-structured linguistic activities.

Sparse transcription avoids segmenting the input on the way to recognizing words; after all, hard boundaries do not exist in the speech stream (Ostendorf, 1999). A sparse transcription is represented as an audio collection, a lexicon, and a collection of tokens that pair lexical entries with locations in the speech stream. For each such token, we keep track of whether it has been confirmed by a speaker.

The ultimate aim of sparse transcription is conventional, dense transcription. However, the intermediate products are useful: a lexicon with confirmed examples from the corpus; and a corpus indexed by terms of interest. These early outputs support oral language learning and access to the content of informal audio collections.

We envisage a context where a background process, a machine in the loop, continually detects putative new tokens of words, leveraging the lexicon and the grammar, presenting them for human confirmation. We anticipate a deployment of our solution inside a collaborative transcription system, increasing the quantity and quality of transcriptions in the early, bootstrapping stage of language work.

2.2 Local Word Discovery

The new task of "local word discovery" was proposed by Lane and Bird (2021) to complement the word spotting described in section 2.1 above. They observe that, for morphologically complex languages, a lexicon consists of morphemes, not full words, avoiding the combinatoric explosion of the vocabulary. Accordingly, we spot lexemes (morphs instead of words), and just require additional computational support to expand confirmed morph tokens into full words. They provide a baseline implementation, a finite state morphological analyzer, which recognizes morphotactically valid words conditioned on a previously confirmed morph together with its left and right phonemic context (See Figure 1).

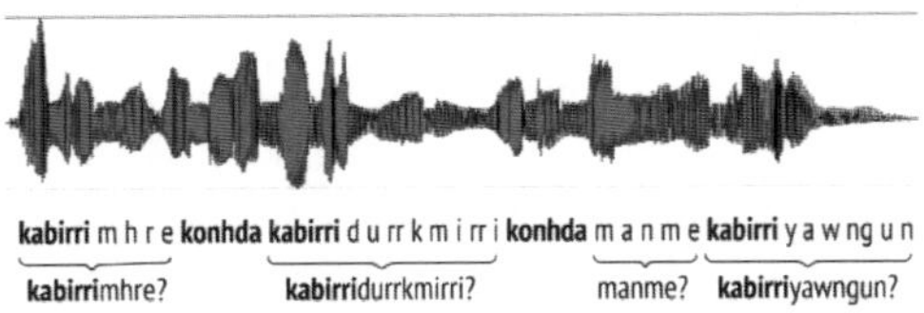

Figure 1: Local word discovery seeks to discover words at the locus of known lexemes.

The phone recognizer is not, as Bird (2020) warns, used to create output for a linguist to post-edit. Rather, it is used as an intermediate representation of the speech, guiding the local word discovery model as it generates plausible word candidates.

A weakness of local word discovery is that it requires explicit alignment of the known lexemes with the phone sequence. The present work addresses this shortcoming by proposing a finite state solution which accepts a phone string and an ordered list of known lexemes as input, and handles the alignment of lexemes to phones implicitly as it generates predictions. This solution relieves the original local word discovery algorithm of its dependency on manual alignment.

2.3 Finite State Morphological Analysis

Finite state methods remain central to computational analysis of morphologically complex languages. Beesley and Karttunen (2003) give a thorough treatment of patterns for finite state modeling of morphology. FSTs continue to play an integral role in the morphological analysis of complex languages, from field grammars (Lane and Bird, 2019) to extensive multi-year projects (Harrigan et al., 2017; Arppe et al., 2017; Schmirler et al., 2017; Snoek et al., 2014), to robust neural models trained on data generated by an FST (Schwartz et al., 2019; Moeller et al., 2018; Lane and Bird, 2020a). Over the years, several finite state toolkits have become prevalent in research, including FOMA (Hulden, 2009) and HFST (Lindén et al., 2009).

2.4 Optimality Theory

Since the 1970's it has been accepted that phonological and syntactic processes can be influenced by constraints on the output of a grammar (McCarthy, 2007). Optimality theory (OT) arose as is a framework for modeling linguistic well-formedness by maximizing the harmonization of ranked constraints (Prince and Smolensky, 2004). In short, OT provides a formalism for flexible ranked constraints on the output of a process. Model output can be optimized by ordering constraints by their relative importance.

The process works as follows. A function GEN generates all possible output candidates given a particular input, or lexical, underlying form. Then all candidates are marked for any violations of the constraints. Finally, an evaluation function EVAL filters out candidates which violate constraints. The candidates which violate the fewest high-ranking constraints are said to be the most harmonic. Suboptimal candidates are culled.

The application of OT to specific input is expressed in a *tableau*, a visual representation of generated candidates (GEN) and the selection of optimal candidates (EVAL) (see Fig. 2).

/input/	Constraint 1	Constraint 2	Constraint 3
Candidate 1	*!		
Candidate 2		*!	
→ Candidate 3			*

Figure 2: Sample OT tableau: candidates are marked for violations of constraints ranked from left to right. Candidates violating more highly-ranked constraints are rejected in favor of those which only violate lesser constraints. Chosen candidates are marked with an arrow.

In this example, some input has prompted the generation of several candidates (column 1). We also see that three constraints have been chosen and ordered according to importance, such that *Constraint 1* $\gg$ *Constraint 2* $\gg$ *Constraint 3* (row 1). The candidates are marked for violations of various constraints with asterisks (columns 2-4). To identify the optimal candidate, we examine the violations marked in the columns from left to right. When a violation occurs, the cell is marked with an exclamation mark. So long as other, viable candidates remain, the current candidate is removed from consideration. After the EVAL process is complete, the optimal candidates are those which violated the fewest, most minimal constraints.

Ellison (1994) showed how OT can be implemented using finite state transducers, so long as three requirements are met: all constraints are binary; the output of GEN is a regular set; and all constraints are regular. For the present application, the GEN function, a morphological transducer, is regular. Equally, the transducers which count violations of phone matches can be converted into a suite of binary, regular transducers.

3 Available Resources

Low-resource languages are not necessarily understudied; many have significant description. This work benefits from an existing finite state morphological analyzer (Lane and Bird, 2019). We use it as an acceptor of morphotactically valid strings in the language, combining canonical lexemes with noisy phone recognizer output.

Additionally, it is common for linguists to maintain a bilingual lexicon, and a corpus of up to 10k words of human-transcribed speech. The computational model described in the following section incorporates these resources. We define two lexicon classes: "topical" words, semantically relevant to the audio we are transcribing, and "attested" words, those known to exist in the overall corpus.

Finally, recent advances in phone recognition have made it possible to train or fine-tune models capable of producing phone sequences from audio (Adams, 2017; Li et al., 2020). Allosaurus is a pretrained universal phone recognizer which allows for language-specific fine-tuning. We obtained the fine-tuned model of (Lane and Bird, 2021) and used it to automatically generate noisy phone sequences from field recordings of Kunwinjku speakers.

4 Joint Alignment and Local Word Discovery

The goal of the proposed local word discovery model is to give useful signal to the transcriber in the form of full word suggestions–which may be completely or partially correct–conditioned on known lexemes provided by the transcriber. Equally, we would like the model to be able to provide high confidence suggestions when possible, and back off to cast a wider net when necessary.

In this section we propose a finite state implementation of local word discovery which accomplishes this, while also incorporating implicit alignment. The GEN function takes a phone string and an ordered list of known lexemes, converts them to FSTs, and produces a list of candidate strings marked for constraint violations. The EVAL function converts these candidate strings to FSTs, and passes them through a cascade of constraints, implemented as FSTs and combined using lenient composition (see Fig. 3).

We employ three types of constraint: (a) anchored – these constraints are anchored to the beginning or end of the phone string; (b) topical – a lexical constraint consisting of words already discovered in the recording we are transcribing; (c) attested – a lexical constraint consisting of words which are attested in the language.[1]

We give more detail about the function of each of these components in the following sections. The Python implementation is available[2].

4.1 GEN

The responsibility of the GEN function is to produce a list of candidate strings which could plausibly be completions of the input anchor lexemes. In this section we describe an implementation of the different pieces of this function in detail.

Input The GEN module requires as input an ordered list of *known lexemes*, and *phone string*. Known lexemes are the anchor morphs, partial words, or full words which the transcriber has recognized in the audio. The phone string comes from access to a phone recognizer, fine-tuned for the target language. We use the Allosaurus model from (Lane and Bird, 2021), which was fine-tuned on 79 minutes of Kunwinjku field recordings and which achieved a 31.8% average word error rate in a 6-fold cross-validation.

Additionally as input we require, for each utterance, an ordered list of orthographic strings. These are the forms that have already been identified in the utterance, the "known lexemes". For example, a linguist might be able to recognize the top N most frequent morphs in the language, and write

[1] In practice, the attested constraints can be spread across multiple lexical buckets according to probability estimations.

[2] http://cdu-tell.gitlab.io/tech-resources/

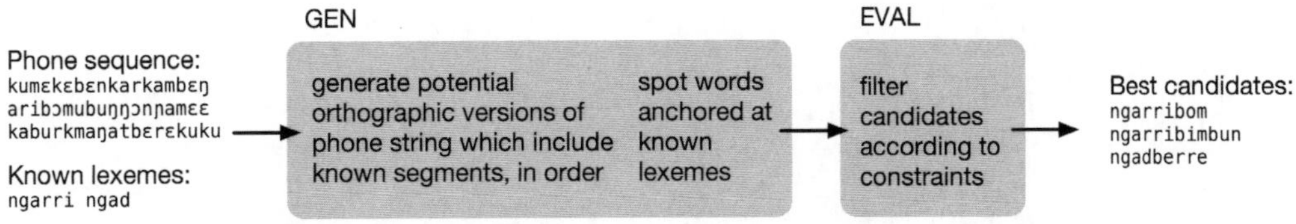

Figure 3: High-level view of local word discovery with implicit alignment.

them out in the order that they hear them in a particular utterance. See lines 1 - 6 of Figure 5 for the definition of input FSTs which would ideally be composed dynamically with the input in a real local word discovery system.

Alignment and Candidate Generation The phone input string is converted into an FST which recognizes and transduces the original string. This FST is composed with an FST which converts phones to their possible orthographic realizations. We automatically construct an FST which transduces the known lexemes into a string of the same ordered lexemes interspersed with zero or more of any character. The XFST code on line 17 of Fig. 5 defines the FST which accepts a list of lexemes and transduces all possible strings which include the lexemes interspersed with arbitrary characters.

The lower side of this relation represents the space of all possible alignments of known lexemes to the phone string. This FST can be composed with edit distance FSTs to transduce the language of candidate string alignments, allowing for alignment of known lexemes with up to N insertion/deletions of flexibility. For example, consider the utterance in (1).

In (1a), we have no known lexemes, and have just identified *kabirri* "they" and *manme* "food." In the next iteration, *kabirri* and *manme* are known lexemes, and we have identified *durrkmirri* "work." Thanks to the implicit alignment in (1b), we see that *kabirri* has been aligned to a less optimal position (requiring the insertion of *a*), in order to accommodate *durrkmirri*.

As the number of known lexemes grows, the potential number of insertions and deletions required to produce valid alignment candidates also grows. Accordingly, we allow greater edit distance for as the length and number of known lexemes grows: 1 edit per known segment of length 1-3 characters, and 2 edits for each longer segment. Our edit distance FST is a minor variation of the pattern set out by Hulden (2013) (e.g., see Fig. 5, lines 18-19).

Phone string: kbiriturkmarɛɲkabiriutuɟmanmɛbɛtbɛrɛ

Known lexemes: kabirri, kabirri

Gold Transcription: kabirridurrkmirri kabirridudjeng manme bedberre

	Anchored	Attested	Topical	Edit Violations
manme	*!			
→ kabirridurrkmirri^			*!	*
birridurrkmi^	*!	*	*	*
birridurrkmarrinj^^	*!	*	*	**
→ kabirridi^			*!	*
kabirridurrkma^		*!	*	*
kabirridu^^		*!	*	**
→ kabirridung^^			*!	**

Figure 4: Constraint tableau for local word discovery with implicit alignment.

After having composed the FST which accepts a phone string and known lexemes as input and transduces all possible variants of the phone string with known lexemes aligned, we compose it with a series of FSTs which recognizes and transduces any word licensed by the morphological FST, allowing any characters to the left or right. This word discovery block can also be altered to allow for some edit distance in order to widen the range of possible licensed words recognized by the morphological analyzer FST (e.g., see Fig. 5, lines 29-32).

Note that depending on which edit distance path is taken, we can append a corresponding tag (In our case the "^" character) to mark how many edit violations were required to produce a particular word candidate (See Fig. 5, lines 24-25, 30-31).

4.2 EVAL

The EVAL function filters candidates according to prioritized constraints, assuming an FST that accepts a phone string and a list of known lexemes, and produces full word candidates marked for edit distance violations (see Fig. 4).

Constraints

In optimality theory, constraints are prioritized conditions that must be maximally satisfied in order to select the optimal candidate set. Optimality theory is traditionally applied to filter for linguistic well-

```
# Set up Lexicons and Mappings as FSTs
define LEXICON [ k u m e kk e | ng a rr i b o m | n a m e kk e | ng a d b e rr e ];
define PHONESTR [k u m k ɛ b ɛ n k a r k a m b ɛ ŋ r b ɔ m ɲ a m ɛ ɛ k a b u r k m a ŋ a t b ɛ r ɛ k u k u];
define LEXEMES [X k u X ng a rr i X ng a d X];
define LEXEMESB [k u | ng a rr i | ng a d];
define TOPICAL [b i m | k u kk u | b i m b o m];
define ATTESTED [k u m e kk e | ng a rr i b o m | ng a d b e rr e];
define PHONES2ORTH  b -> [ b | bb ] .o.
                    ɲ -> [ nj ] .o.
                    ŋ -> [ ng ] .o.
                    n -> [ n ] .o.
                    t -> [ d ] .o.
                    k -> [ k | kk ] .o.
                    d -> [ t | d ] .o.
                    ...
                    i -> [ i ];

 define LexemePattern [[LEXEMES .o. [X -> ?*]].i].u;
 define Edit1 [?* [?:0|0:?|?:?-?] ?*]^<2;
 define Edit2 [?* [?:0|0:?|?:?-?] ?*]^<3;

 # GEN: Generate alignment candidates
 define OrthStrs  [PHONESTR .o. PHONES2ORTH];
 define Edit0Align [[?]* LexemePattern [?]*]["^"]*;
 define Edit1Align [[?]* [ Edit1 .o. LexemePattern] [?]*][0:"^"];
 define Edit2Align [[?]* [ Edit2 .o. LexemePattern] [?]*][0:"^"][0:"^"];
 define AlignedOrth [OrthStrs .o. [ Edit0Align | Edit1Align | Edit2Align ]];

 # GEN: Generate word candidates from alignment candidates
 define Edit0Discover [[?:0]* LEXICON [?:0]*]["^"]*;
 define Edit1Discover [[?:0]* [Edit1 .o. LEXICON] [?:0]*][0:"^"];
 define Edit2Discover [[?:0]* [Edit2 .o. LEXICON] [?:0]*][0:"^"][0:"^"];
 define DiscoverWords [AlignedOrth .o. [ Edit0Discover | Edit1Discover | Edit2Discover]];

 # EVAL: Evaluate word candidates
 define AnchoredWords [?+ LEXEMESB] | [LEXEMESB ?+] | [?+ LEXEMESB ?+];
 define TopicalWords [?* TOPICAL ?*];
 define AttestedWords [?* ATTESTED ?*];
 define edit1Words [[?-"^"]* ["^"]^<2 ];
 define edit2Words [[?-"^"]* ["^"]^<3 ];

 regex DiscoverWords  .O. AnchoredWords
                      .O. AttestedWords
                      .O. TopicalWords
                      .O. edit2Words
                      .O. edit1Words;
```

Figure 5: Minimal example of local word discovery with implicit alignment. NB `LEXEMES` and `PHONESTR` FSTs would typically be built on the fly using input to the algorithm. For this reason, our final algorithm implements the logic presented here with the HFST Python bindings, enabling parts of the network to be compiled at input time.

formedness. However, in the case of local word discovery, grammaticality is already captured by GEN, and the morphological FST. Therefore, we only need to constrain candidates on pragmatics grounds: what context can we leverage to elevate some words over the others? Through a trial and error process typical of OT, we identified the following ranking: *anchored* ≫ *attested* ≫ *topical* ≫ edit distance.

Anchored candidates are words which are attached to a known segment provided by the user. The model could easily hallucinate candidates across the entire phone string. However, such a broad search with loose edit distance parameters generates many spurious candidates. It is preferable to focus search on candidates for which we already have strong priors.

Attested candidates are words which are attested in some form across a wider corpus of language. We represent attested candidates which occur in a lexicon of the top $N\%$ most frequently words drawn from a corpus of public texts published in Kunwinjku: a bible translation, a set of 45 Kunwinjku children's books accessed from AIATSIS (AIATSIS Mura Collections Catalogue, 2021), and the example sentences scraped from the Kunwinjku dictionary (Bininj Kunwok Regional Language Centre, 2021). For the model evaluated in this work, we set N to 30%.

Topical candidates are words which have already been transcribed from audio related to the current audio. This lexicon grows over time, but its scope should remain topically limited to relevant themes and locations of the audio we are currently annotating. In this work, the audio we are transcribing comes from a tour of the outstation of Kabulwarnamyo. We have previous recordings which have been transcribed with other speakers giving similar tours, and so we sample a small set of words from these to simulate a small set of 8 words to seed the *topical* lexicon.

Edit Violations are the final and lowest-priority of the constraints. Essentially, if we arrive at a set of words which are already anchored, attested, and topical, then we would further filter that result set by taking those with the least number of edit distance violations.

These constraints are operationalized in the EVAL function through the use of lenient composition, a finite state operator that allows strings to violate constraints as long as there are no other strings which do not violate that constraint. That is, a set of string candidates can be passed through a chain of leniently-composed FSTs which check for adherence to their individual constraints. At each successive state, strings which violate the constraint are filtered out, and the remaining strings are passed to the next constraint. If no more strings are able to pass a filter, then the last viable set of strings is returned as the result set (Karttunen, 1998).

5 Model Evaluation and Results

The objective of this model is to provide a reasonable set of word candidates which lead to correct transcriptions. As such, any model suggestions which correctly predict subword units beyond the anchor lexemes can be useful for helping the transcriber discern the full word they are hearing, as they interactively poll the model. Accordingly, we chose to evaluate the performance of this model by automatically simulating a first pass at transcribing 126 utterances of the test set. These 126 utterances are recorded audio segmented by breath group, from a tour of Kabulwarnamyo, conducted in Kunwinjku.

The input of the model requires a phone string, and an ordered list of known lexemes. As already mentioned, we use the Allosaurus model fine-tuned for Kunwinjku of (Lane and Bird, 2021). Similarly, we adopt their sparse transcription data preparation method: we simulate a sparse transcription of the audio by selecting a vocabulary of the top 20 morphs occurring in the training set, and use that vocabulary to manually annotate the test set. To see how this works, suppose that the test set includes an audio file (2).

(2) birri-wam balanda birri-bo-ngu-ni
they-went white.person they-liquid-eat-PI
'the white people went off drinking'

The corresponding prepared sparse transcription would be the unaligned, ordered list of morphs from the "known" vocabulary, i.e., *birri*, *balanda*, *birri*.

Using these sparse transcriptions and the automatically derived phone strings, we fed the test set to the local word discovery model to generate a list of candidate words anchored at the locus of the known lexemes. In this way, we found that 12.7% of all predictions across all utterances were correct full word predictions. Additionally, 38.2% of all model suggestions were partially correct, i.e., a substring of the suggested word attached to the anchor segment was correct, and thus a useful signal for the transcriber to decide how to continue transcribing the word (Fig. 7).

On the utterance level, 57.9% of result sets contained correct full word suggestions, and 66.7% contained correct partial word suggestions. In total, 86.5% of utterance-level result sets contained correct full or partial word suggestions. A sample of these results can be seen in Fig. 6.

6 Discussion

The key feature of this model is that we drop manual lexeme-to-phone alignment, and instead perform alignment on the fly, incorporating newly identified lexemes. This is illustrated in (1), where newly identified morphemes for each iteration are marked in red.

This innovation has an important consequence for the transcription process: it can be *iterative*. Each time the linguist and/or speaker revisit an utterance, they consider a new set of suggestions for building the transcription out from known lexemes where the model has taken care of working out where everything fits. They may also posit entirely new lexemes and add them to the lexicon. For each new lexeme, the user only needs to indicate their relative position with respect to existing lexemes.

For each new visit to an utterance, the lexicon is in an expanded state due to transcription of other utterances, and the model makes new suggestions.

The model handles some subtle issues in transcription. For example, when a morph appears multiple times in an utterance, as we see for *kabirri* "they" (1). When a transcriber adds a lexeme, the model assigns it to the best location, but only for the purpose of discovering words anchored at this lexeme (1a). When the transcriber identifies a new lexeme, e.g. *durrkmirri* "work", the previously

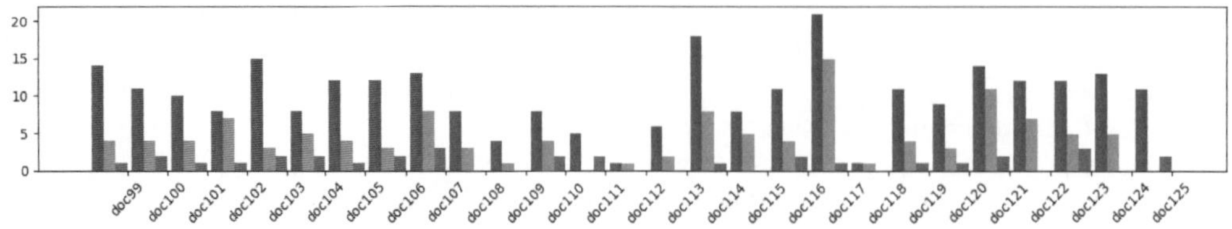

Figure 6: Sample of test set utterances with #suggestions by model (blue); #correct partial word suggestions (orange); #correct full word suggestions (green).

Number of utterances	126
% predictions full correct	12.7
% predictions partial correct	38.2
% docs with full correct	57.9
% docs with partial correct	66.7
% docs with any correct	86.5

Figure 7: LWD-A Test Set Statistics

identified lexeme is aligned elsewhere (1b). Further suggestions–by the human transcriber or an automatic word spotter–identify a second instance of *kabirri* (1c).

Alongside these benefits are some shortcomings. First, if a transcriber is mistaken about the identity of a lexeme, the model will not be able to come up with better suggestions for that locus, except in the unlikely event that there is another locus where that incorrect lexeme can be aligned. Second, the model may generate suggestions for a given anchor lexeme, when a user wants to work on a different part of the utterance. Here, the user may need to accept high priority suggestions (if they are correct) and wait for a later iteration to get model suggestions for other parts of the utterance. Third, thanks to the iterative nature of this approach, the precision and recall of the model for a given utterance depends on how high we are in the constraint hierarchy when results are returned. High priority constraints are more precise, with results sets of 1 or 2 candidates (varying on the size of the topical lexicon). Low priority constraints contain edit distance-based variations on the source signal, and therefore can grow quite large with as a function of uncertainty.

This variability with precision and recall leads to a further benefit. The model is able to prioritize precision when possible, while backing off to recall when necessary. Accordingly, for our test data, the average number of predictions per utterance is just 6.5, compared to an average of 64.1 predictions per utterance of the non-constraint based model of Lane and Bird (2021).

A further shortcoming of our approach is that we must compile unique FSTs at runtime. This means we cannot precompile the network with LEXC and FOMA or HFST compilers, but must use Python bindings, and compile FSTs dynamically with each new input. This could be prohibitively slow in some instances, as complexity increases exponentially with the size of the phone stream and known segment lists. A solution is to add a preprocessing step: utterances are already segmented from the original audio using silence; any overlong utterances are further split on confirmed full words.

7 Conclusion

We have proposed a novel approach to collaborative transcription, which works with locally available resources and human capacities. In particular, local Indigenous participation is not reduced to laborious and unmotivated phone transcription, but focuses on the identification of keywords in connected speech. These may be relevant to a concurrent cultural activity, or to language learning, in which the meaning of words in context is of more interest than their phonemic representation. The results suggest that this model does well in leveraging a computational grammar to give meaningful, interactive signal in a collaborative transcription context. This model improves on previous local word discovery models in that it is able to suggest words while performing alignment implicitly. We anticipate that this approach will integrate with interactive, collaborative transcription systems, such as (Lane and Bird, 2020b). We also hope to have shown a way of bridging language data collection to locally-motivated language work.

Ethical Considerations

This research has been approved by traditional owners in the communities where it was conducted, and the board of Warddeken, the Aboriginal land management company which hosted the research. It is covered by a research permit from the Northern Land Council and by human research ethics approval of Charles Darwin University. The authors have made several visits to an Aboriginal communities over several years, working closely with elders and traditional owners in pursuing their agenda for the future of their languages.

References

Oliver Adams. 2017. *Automatic Understanding of Unwritten Languages*. Ph.D. thesis, University of Melbourne.

AIATSIS Mura Collections Catalogue. 2021. Accessed 2021-12-10. [link].

Antti Arppe, Christopher Cox, Mans Hulden, Jordan Lachler, Sjur N Moshagen, Miikka Silfverberg, and Trond Trosterud. 2017. Computational modeling of verbs in Dene languages: The case of Tsuut'ina. In *Proceedings of the 2016 Dene Languages Conference*, pages 51–69. Alaska Native Language Center, University of Alaska, Fairbanks.

Kenneth R. Beesley and Lauri Karttunen. 2003. *Finite-State Morphology: Xerox Tools and Techniques*. Stanford: CSLI.

Bininj Kunwok Regional Language Centre. 2021. Bininj Kunwok Dictionary. `njamed.com`. Accessed 2021-07-19.

Steven Bird. 2020. Sparse transcription. *Computational Linguistics*, 46:713–744.

Luc Bouquiaux and Jacqueline M. C. Thomas. 1992. *Studying and describing unwritten languages*. Dallas: Summer Institute of Linguistics.

Terry Crowley. 2007. *Field Linguistics: A Beginner's Guide*. Oxford University Press.

T. Mark Ellison. 1994. Phonological derivation in Optimality Theory. In *COLING 1994 Volume 2: The 15th International Conference on Computational Linguistics*, pages 1007–1013.

Joshua A. Fishman, editor. 2001. *Can Threatened Languages be Saved?: Reversing Language Shift, Revisited: A 21st Century Perspective*. Multilingual Matters.

Lenore Grenoble and Lindsay Whaley. 2006. *Saving Languages: An Introduction to Language Revitalization*. Cambridge University Press.

Ken Hale. 2001. Ulwa (Southern Sumu): the beginnings of a language research project. In Paul Newman and Martha Ratliff, editors, *Linguistic Fieldwork*, pages 76–101. Cambridge University Press.

Atticus Harrigan, Katherine Schmirler, Antti Arppe, Lene Antonsen, Trond Trosterud, and Arok Wolvengrey. 2017. Learning from the computational modelling of Plains Cree verbs. *Morphology*, 27(4):565–598.

Leanne Hinton and Kenneth Hale, editors. 2001. *The Green Book of Language Revitalization in Practice*. Academic Press.

Mans Hulden. 2009. Foma: a finite-state compiler and library. In *Proceedings of the Demonstrations Session at EACL 2009*, pages 29–32, Athens, Greece. Association for Computational Linguistics.

Mans Hulden. 2013. Advanced finite-state techniques tutorial. `http://clt.gu.se/sites/clt.gu.se/files/mkp/clttutorial.pdf`. Accessed 2020-01-07.

Lauri Karttunen. 1998. The proper treatment of optimality in computational phonology. In *Finite State Methods in Natural Language Processing*.

Alexander D King. 2015. Add language documentation to any ethnographic project in six steps. *Anthropology Today*, 31:8–12.

William Lane and Steven Bird. 2019. Towards a robust morphological analyzer for kunwinjku. In *Proceedings of the The 17th Annual Workshop of the Australasian Language Technology Association*, pages 1–9, Sydney, Australia. Australasian Language Technology Association.

William Lane and Steven Bird. 2020a. Bootstrapping techniques for polysynthetic morphological analysis. In *Proceedings of the 58th Annual Meeting of the Association for Computational Linguistics*, pages 6652–6661, Online. Association for Computational Linguistics.

William Lane and Steven Bird. 2020b. Interactive word completion for morphologically complex languages. In *Proceedings of the 28th International Conference on Computational Linguistics*, pages 4600–4611, Barcelona, Spain (Online). International Committee on Computational Linguistics.

William Lane and Steven Bird. 2021. Local word discovery for interactive transcription. In *Proceedings of the 2021 Conference on Empirical Methods in Natural Language Processing*, pages 2058–2067. Association for Computational Linguistics.

Xinjian Li, Siddharth Dalmia, Juncheng Li, Matthew Lee, Patrick Littell, Jiali Yao, Antonios Anastasopoulos, David R. Mortensen, Graham Neubig, Alan W Black, and Florian Metze. 2020. Universal phone recognition with a multilingual allophone system. In *Proceedings of the International Conference on*

Acoustics, Speech and Signal Processing, pages 8249–8253. IEEE.

Krister Lindén, Miikka Silfverberg, and Tommi Pirinen. 2009. Hfst tools for morphology–an efficient open-source package for construction of morphological analyzers. In *International Workshop on Systems and Frameworks for Computational Morphology*, pages 28–47. Springer.

John J McCarthy. 2007. What is optimality theory? 1. *Language and Linguistics Compass*, 1(4):260–291.

Felicity Meakins, Jenny Green, and Myfany Turpin. 2018. *Understanding Linguistic Fieldwork*. Routledge.

Sarah Moeller, Ghazaleh Kazeminejad, Andrew Cowell, and Mans Hulden. 2018. A neural morphological analyzer for Arapaho verbs learned from a finite state transducer. In *Proceedings of the Workshop on Computational Modeling of Polysynthetic Languages*, pages 12–20, Santa Fe, New Mexico, USA. Association for Computational Linguistics.

Paul Newman and Martha Ratliff. 2001. Introduction. In Paul Newman and Martha Ratliff, editors, *Linguistic Fieldwork*. Cambridge University Press.

NHMRC. 2018. *Ethical conduct in research with Aboriginal and Torres Strait Islander Peoples and communities: Guidelines for researchers and stakeholders*. National Health and Medical Research Council.

Walter Ong. 1982. *Orality and Literacy: The Technologizing of the Word*. Routledge.

Mari Ostendorf. 1999. Moving beyond the 'beads-on-a-string' model of speech. In *Proceedings of the IEEE Automatic Speech Recognition and Understanding Workshop*, pages 79–84.

Alan Prince and Paul Smolensky. 2004. *Optimality Theory: Constraint interaction in generative grammar*. John Wiley & Sons.

Katherine Schmirler, Antti Arppe, Trond Trosterud, and Lene Antonsen. 2017. Computational modelling of Plains Cree syntax: A constraint grammar approach to verbs and arguments in a Plains Cree corpus. In *49th Algonquian Conference, Montreal, QC*.

Lane Schwartz, Emily Chen, Benjamin Hunt, and Sylvia Schreiner. 2019. Bootstrapping a neural morphological analyzer for St. Lawrence Island Yupik from a finite-state transducer. In *Proceedings of the Workshop on Computational Methods for Endangered Languages*, pages 87–96.

Conor Snoek, Dorothy Thunder, Kaidi Loo, Antti Arppe, Jordan Lachler, Sjur Moshagen, and Trond Trosterud. 2014. Modeling the noun morphology of Plains Cree. In *Proceedings of the 2014 Workshop on the Use of Computational Methods in the Study of Endangered Languages*, pages 34–42. Association for Computational Linguistics.

David P Wilkins. 2000. Even with the best of intentions...: Some pitfalls in the fight for linguistic and cultural survival (one view of the Australian experience). *As linguas amazonicas hoje: the Amazonian languages today*, pages 61–83.

Anthony C. Woodbury. 2003. Defining documentary linguistics. *Language Documentation and Description*, 1:35–51.

Corpus-Guided Contrast Sets for Morphosyntactic Feature Detection in Low-Resource English Varieties

Tessa Masis *they/them/theirs* **Anissa Neal** *she/her/hers* **Lisa Green** *she/her/hers* **Brendan O'Connor** *he/him/his*

University of Massachusetts Amherst
{tmasis,brenocon}@cs.umass.edu
{anneal,lgreen}@linguist.umass.edu

Abstract

The study of language variation examines how language varies between and within different groups of speakers, shedding light on how we use language to construct identities and how social contexts affect language use. A common method is to identify instances of a certain linguistic feature—say, the zero copula construction—in a corpus, and analyze the feature's distribution across speakers, topics, and other variables, to either gain a qualitative understanding of the feature's function or systematically measure variation. In this paper, we explore the challenging task of automatic morphosyntactic feature detection in low-resource English varieties. We present a human-in-the-loop approach to generate and filter effective contrast sets via corpus-guided edits. We show that our approach improves feature detection for both Indian English and African American English, demonstrate how it can assist linguistic research, and release our fine-tuned models for use by other researchers.

1 Introduction

Linguistic *features*—such as specific phonological, syntactic, or lexical phenomena that may be associated with a language variety—are widely used by sociolinguists to quantify linguistic variation between speakers through feature frequency measurements (Renn and Terry, 2009; Grieser, 2019; Craig and Washington, 2006), even if subject to certain limitations (Green, 2017). Since manual annotation is limited due to the required expert human labor, automatic methods are a valuable alternative (Grieve et al., 2011; Jones, 2015; Eisenstein, 2015; Nguyen et al., 2016). However, accurately detecting morphosyntactic features (e.g. Figure 1) remains an open challenge, especially in informal genres such as transcripts and social media, and in low resource nonstandard languages. We explore fine-tuning pretrained language models (LMs) for utterance-level classification of a feature by training on a *contrast set*—a small collection of positive and negative examples that are highly similar—as recently introduced by Demszky et al. (2021).

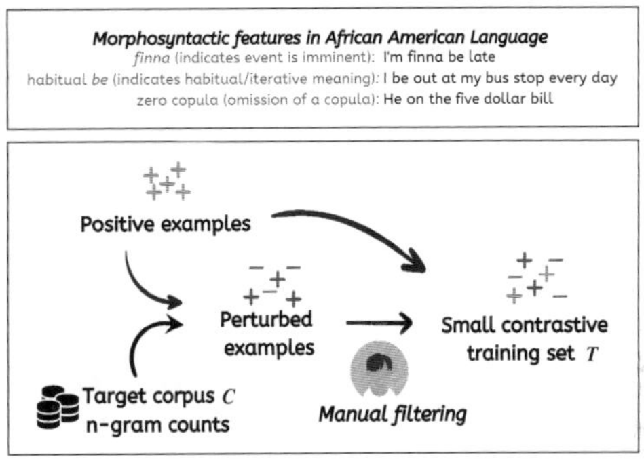

Figure 1: Top: Example features. Bottom: Our approach to generate contrast sets for feature detection.

Our work makes the following contributions:

- We propose a method for generating morphosyntactically contrastive training data, combining corpus-driven edits and human-in-the-loop filtering (§4).
- We evaluate our method's ability to detect features against new baselines on three datasets, encompassing two Englishes (Indian English (IndE) and African American English (AAE)) and two centuries of speakers, and show that our best method outperforms prior work by up to 16 points in Prec@100 scores (§5).
- For further validation, we confirm and extend the findings of sociolinguistic studies of AAE which use manual feature annotation to examine if feature use aligns with social factors like age and gender (§6).
- Finally, we release training data and models for detecting 10 features in IndE and 17 in AAE.[1]

[1]https://github.com/slanglab/CGEdit

Proceedings of the first workshop on NLP applications to field linguistics, pages 11–25
July 5–10, 2020. ©2020 Association for Computational Linguistics
https://doi.org/10.26615/978-954-452-056-4_002

2 Related Work

Feature detection. Detecting morphosyntactic features in low-resource domains presents significant challenges. Rule-based approaches have used sequences of unigrams and POS tags to identify syntactic features (Blodgett et al., 2016), but many features cannot be defined by sequences and the tags may be unreliable. More recently, machine learning has been used for feature detection by training domain-specific LMs with synthetically augmented data (Santiago et al., 2022), fine-tuning pretrained LMs with contrast sets (Demszky et al., 2021), or manually filtering results from noisy classifiers (Austen, 2017). While prior work has only considered one language variety at a time and primarily evaluated with labeled test sets, we examine performance on multiple language varieties and analyze external sociolinguistic validity.

Contrast set generation. Manual generation of contrast sets has mostly been used for semantic tasks (Staliūnaitė and Bonfil, 2017; Mahler et al., 2017; Gardner et al., 2020), and occasionally for morphosyntactic tasks (Demszky et al., 2021). Unlike these approaches, our proposed method generates a *morphosyntactically diverse* contrast set via a corpus-guided edit system. Data augmentation methods for automatic generation of contrast sets include random edits (Smith and Eisner, 2005; Alleman et al., 2021), which cannot target specific linguistic features, or informed edits (Burlot and Yvon, 2017; Sennrich, 2017; Gulordava et al., 2018; Miao et al., 2020; Ross et al., 2021), which require syntactic or semantic annotations that are not easily available for datasets with nonstandard languages.

3 Task and Data

3.1 Morphosyntactic feature detection

Given a training set T, target corpus C, and morphosyntactic features F, for each $f \in F$ we model

$$P(f_x = 1 \mid T, x), \tag{1}$$

where $f_x \in \{0, 1\}$ indicates the utterance $x \in C$ contains the feature when $f_x = 1$. An utterance may contain multiple features.

3.2 Language Varieties and Data

We consider two English varieties, IndE and AAE, each with their own target corpora C and feature inventories F; see Appendix A for feature lists.

Indian English. The International Corpus of English (ICE) (Greenbaum and Nelson, 1996) is a collection of national and regional English varieties, and contains IndE material produced after 1989. The ICE-India subcorpus that our study uses is the complete subset of spontaneous spoken dialogues (21,759 utterances). We use manual annotations of 10 syntactic features from Lange (2012).

African American English. We use two unlabeled AAE corpora. The first is the Corpus of Regional African American Language (CORAAL) (Kendall and Farrington, 2021), which contains sociolinguistic interviews with AAE speakers from 1968-2017 from six US sites (152,069 utterances). The second is Born in Slavery: Slave Narratives from the Federal Writers' Project, 1936-38 (FWP) (Library of Congress, 2001), a digital archive containing over 2,300 ex-slave narratives, with speakers from 17 US states (148,018 utterances).[2]

We examine 17 AAE features, sourced from Green (2002) and Koenecke et al. (2020); examples of three features are in Figure 1, and a complete list is in Appendix A. During evaluation, we manually annotated the top 100 utterances per AAE feature, for each corpus, for the Prec@100 scores in §5.

4 CGEDIT: Corpus-Guided Edits

4.1 Motivation

Our method starts with a seed set of positive examples illustrating a feature, then uses corpus n-gram statistics to generate proposed negative (and additional positive) examples, which require manual filtering by the user to define the final training set. A major motivation is speed and ease of use—it is easier to filter candidate examples than to manually write all the examples, as in Demszky et al. (2021).

At the same time, we believe negative examples should be intelligently synthesized. A morphosyntactic feature is beholden to its syntactic constraints (i.e. word order, co-occurrence requirements); if a sentence does not follow these constraints then it is not an instance of the feature (Wilson and Mihalicek, 2011, Ch. 5.2). For example, an instance of zero copula must have a noun phrase immediately followed by a predicate and must not have a copula. The positive example in Figure 2 obeys these syntactic constraints while the negatives do

[2]Given authenticity and reliability concerns about FWP (Maynor, 1988; Wolfram, 1990), we primarily use it to evaluate our method, and not to pursue linguistic questions about Early African American English.

not. Unlike previous work which uses constraints to detect or generate positive instances, *we generate negative examples which minimally violate these constraints* to create a contrast set that defines a tight decision boundary. Based on the view that good syntax is largely independent from meaning (Chomsky, 1957), we argue that focusing on syntactic constraint violation is a useful first step. While potentially valuable, semantic-preserving edits are beyond the scope of this work.

4.2 Method

Training data. We briefly describe how the contrast sets are generated (Figure 2; see Appendix B for details). For a single feature, the input is a small set P of 5 positive examples constructed by the authors and an unlabeled target corpus C to compute n-gram statistics. The output is a contrast set T consisting of both P plus semi-synthetic positive and negative examples.

The first step proposes candidate examples by perturbing words in positive examples through corpus-guided local edits. For each overlapping 3-gram t in a positive example p, we perturb it by swapping t for a new 2-, 3-, or 4-gram t' that is both similar to t, and has a high frequency in target corpus C. Similarity is defined as having 0 to 1 subtoken difference between t and t'.[3] This step typically produces 10-50 perturbed examples, which may or may not have the feature. Our corpus-guided edits are effective because they generate plausible sentences with targeted edits, while random edits often propose ungrammatical output.[4]

In the second step, the perturbed examples are manually filtered so that only 2 positive and 3 negative examples are retained for each original p. Both p and the new examples are included in the final training set T. This step takes 30-60 seconds per p, and was performed by the first author.

Models. We fine-tune multiheaded BERT models, where each head is a binary classifier for a single feature (Devlin et al., 2019). We use two sets of models in our experiments, where a set shares a language variety, a feature inventory F, target corpora C (i.e. test set for our results in Table 1), and a BERT variant (*bert-base-uncased* for IndE, *bert-base-cased* for AAE, selected based on preliminary experiments). The only variation between models *within* a set is the approach used to generate the training set T. Models were fine-tuned with cross-entropy loss for 500 epochs using the Adam optimizer, batch size of 64, and learning rate of 10^{-5}, warmed up over the first 150 epochs.[5]

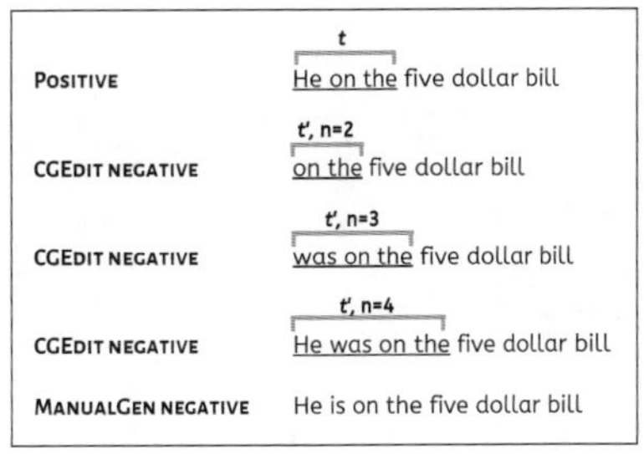

Figure 2: Examples of negative examples generated via our approach, compared to a semantically-matched, manually created example (MANUALGEN).

5 Results and Analysis

Baselines. We compare our approach (which we refer to as CGEDIT) to several baseline methods, all of which take the same seed set of positive examples P then add negative examples to complete the training set. Examples in P were sourced from Demszky et al. (2021) for IndE and crafted by the authors for AAE.

MANUALGEN: The approach used in Demszky et al. (2021). This method involves manually generating negatives by modifying positive examples so they are (1) semantically-similar Mainstream American English versions, and (2) do not have the feature (see Figure 2); see discussion in §4.1. Next, we also test two methods to completely automatically generate negative examples:

AUTOGEN: This approach automatically generates negative examples by dividing a positive example p into n-grams and shuffling the n-grams.

AUTOID: Automatic identification randomly chooses unlabeled examples from target corpus C as the negatives. The assumption that unlabeled examples are negatives with class label noise underpins contrastive learning (Chen et al., 2020) and PU learning methods (Bekker and Davis, 2020).

Overall results. Table 1 presents performance

[3] Specifically, the set difference between subtoken sets $set(t)$ and $set(t')$ must have cardinality 0 or 1; thus a 2-gram t' represents a (sub)token deletion, a 4-gram an insertion, and perturbations may change order as well. Since only a single 3-gram is changed, the resulting perturbed utterance has a low edit distance to the original.

[4] While our n-gram swapping heuristic is straightforward, generating from a C-specific language model could be an interesting alternative in future work.

[5] Early experiments indicated that class-balanced loss did not improve scores.

	ICE-India			CORAAL	FWP
Approach	ROC-AUC	AP	Prec@100	Prec@100	Prec@100
AUTOGEN	68.94	12.63	16.93	-	-
AUTOID	74.90	15.24	17.87	-	-
MANUALGEN	86.83	25.77	31.63	57.88	58.71
AUTOID + MANUALGEN	76.34	19.95	24.30	-	-
CGEDIT	84.92	27.48	32.50	**67.41**	68.00
MANUALGEN + CGEDIT	**88.76**	**29.32**	**35.67**	64.94	**74.35**

Table 1: Area under precision-recall curve (ROC-AUC), average precision (AP), and precision@100 in percentages for feature detection on all three corpora. Results are averages over all features (10 in ICE-India, 17 in CORAAL and FWP). Reported scores for ICE-India are averaged from three runs with different random seeds. Best scores are bolded.

of the proposed approach against baselines and prior work. AUTOGEN and AUTOID perform the worst across metrics. CGEDIT outperforms MANUALGEN, the best prior work on this task, by up to 10 points in Prec@100 scores for both AAE datasets, CORAAL and FWP. Combining the training sets of MANUALGEN and CGEDIT yielded the best performance, consistently outperforming MANUALGEN by about 4 points across metrics in ICE-INDIA and by about 10-15 points in Prec@100 scores for both CORAAL and FWP. These gains can't simply be attributed to more training data, as combining AUTOID and MANUALGEN training sets did not improve performance.

Better performance on AAE corpora may be due to a few variables: a higher number of AAE features means a larger total training set; larger AAE corpora mean more target corpus n-grams; the selected AAE features may be easier to distinguish or more prevalent than the IndE ones. Discrepancies between CORAAL and FWP are likely due to different feature prevalences.

Results by feature. Feature difficulty is similar across approaches; invariant features are easier to detect (i.e. focus *itself* in IndE; *finna* in AAE), while features with long-distance dependencies are more difficult (i.e. double object construction in AAE). See Appendix C for complete results.

6 Replicating Prior Sociolinguistic Work

We recreate three recent studies of CORAAL where original authors manually annotated AAE morphosyntactic features and analyzed correlations between feature frequency and speaker metadata (i.e. gender, region, socioeconomic status). We used the combined MANUALGEN + CGEDIT model and Classify & Count (CC, summing hard classifica-

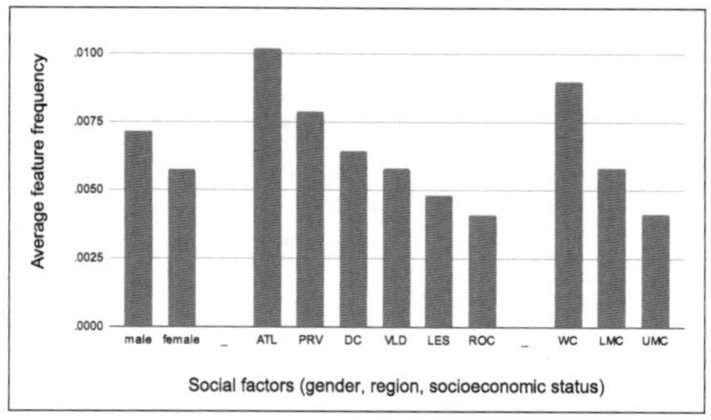

Figure 3: African American English feature variation by speaker's social factor, across all of CORAAL. Regions are Atlanta, GA; Princeville, NC; Washington, DC; Valdosta, GA; Lower East Side, NY; Rochester, NY; socioeconomic classes are Working Class, Lower Middle Class, Upper Middle Class.

tions (Bella et al., 2010)) to calculate per-speaker feature frequency.[6] The same subsets of features and CORAAL were used as in previous work when possible; detailed results are in Appendix C.

Koenecke et al. (2020) annotated 35 morphosyntactic features in 150 utterances. We confirm their conclusions that average feature frequency was lowest in Rochester, followed by DC, then Princeville; and lower among male speakers than female.

Cukor-Avila and Balcazar (2019) looked at 3 features over 14,506 utterances. They qualitatively found considerable variation in feature use between speakers, even when within the same age group. We confirm this quantitatively: standard deviation between speakers within an age group is larger than standard deviation between age group means.

Grieser (2019) examined 14 features over 18,553 utterances. We confirm findings that age and so-

[6]In early experiments we tested the Saerens et al. (2002) EM algorithm and PCC (Bella et al., 2010) to improve frequency estimation, but found few improvements.

cioeconomic status are negatively correlated with feature use. Grieser also found that being male was weakly correlated with feature use; interestingly, our results agree when we look at all 17 features or all of CORAAL, but not when we look at the same feature and data subsets as Grieser. This may indicate how small sample size (in terms of both features and datasets) can skew results.

See Figure 3 for average frequencies of our 17 features in all 152,069 utterances of CORAAL, broken down by several social factors of the speaker. Feature detection at this scale is only possible with automatic methods, and allows researchers to draw more reliable conclusions about language use.

7 Discussion and Future Work

We propose a corpus-driven and manually-filtered approach to generate contrast sets for morphosyntactic feature detection in low-resource language varieties, which may be useful for novel sociolinguistic analysis in future work. This approach may be extendable to datasets with other nonstandard language varieties (e.g. ICE with 14 English varieties (Greenbaum and Nelson, 1996), QADI with 18 Arabic varieties (Abdelali et al., 2021), Corpus del Español with 21 Spanish varieties (Davies, 2016), or Masakhane's African language collection, currently under development (∀ et al., 2020)), in addition to social media corpora, which are largely unlabeled and could benefit from automatic methods.

Additionally, while we only examined automatic identification of noisy negatives, future work might explore automatic identification of reliable negatives by using an apt word representation and distance function to obtain unlabeled examples which are least similar to the positives (Bekker and Davis, 2020). Other extensions might consider adding manual filtering to an automatic identification approach, such as filtering through and identifying the nearest unlabeled examples that are true negatives, instead of identifying reliable (e.g. distant) negatives.

8 Ethical Considerations and Broader Impact

Our objective is to expand the linguistic coverage of NLP tools to include marginalized language varieties, so that they may also benefit from the linguistic analysis made possible by methodological innovation. We hope to aid both sociolinguistic and corpus linguistic researchers studying nonstandard language use.

Since language varieties, including the ones examined in this study, may correlate with the national origin or ethnicity of the speaker and linguistic feature frequency may correlate with social factors, such as gender or socioeconomic status, there is a risk of automatic feature detection being used to infer personal information about a speaker (Kröger et al., 2022; Chancellor et al., 2019; Veronese et al., 2019). Our study has sought to show that there is a correlation between language use and social factors, but does not support any claims about the accuracy or ethics of using linguistic feature frequency to predict a given social factor.

There is not a one-to-one mapping of feature frequency to ethnicity, socioeconomic status, or any other social factor. Two speakers with the same set of social factors may exhibit different feature frequencies; life circumstances do not deterministically produce linguistic competence. In addition, linguistic competence does not deterministically produce feature frequency. Every speaker has the ability to style-shift and thus use linguistic features to varying degrees for a given context, exhibiting a range of feature frequencies throughout their spoken interactions (Sharma, 2017, 2018). There are many factors that may influence observed feature frequency, including pragmatic context, register, topic, relationship between the speakers, relationship to one's own identity, and so on. This complex relationship between language production and external factors should be considered when using this technology.

Acknowledgements

We would like to thank Devyani Sharma for help with accessing the ICE-India corpus and Claudia Lange's annotations, with permission. We would also like to thank the UMass AAE group as well as anonymous reviewers from the First Field Matters Workshop for their helpful comments and feedback. This work was supported by National Science Foundation grants 1845576 and 2042939; any opinions, findings, and conclusions or recommendations expressed in this material are those of the authors and do not necessarily reflect the views of the National Science Foundation.

References

Ahmed Abdelali, Hamdy Mubarak, Younes Samih, Sabit Hassan, and Kareem Darwish. 2021. QADI: Arabic Dialect Identification in the Wild. In *Proceedings of the Sixth Arabic Natural Language Processing Workshop*, pages 1–10, Kyiv, Ukraine (Virtual). Association for Computational Linguistics.

Matteo Alleman, Jonathan Mamou, Miguel A Del Rio, Hanlin Tang, Yoon Kim, and SueYeon Chung. 2021. Syntactic Perturbations Reveal Representational Correlates of Hierarchical Phrase Structure in Pretrained Language Models. In *Proceedings of the 6th Workshop on Representation Learning for NLP (RepL4NLP-2021)*, pages 263–276, Online. Association for Computational Linguistics.

Martha Austen. 2017. "Put the Groceries Up": Comparing Black and White Regional Variation. *American Speech*, 92(3):298–320.

Jessa Bekker and Jesse Davis. 2020. Learning from Positive and Unlabeled Data: A Survey. *Mach. Learn.*, 109(4):719–760.

Antonio Bella, Cesar Ferri, José Hernández-Orallo, and María José Ramírez-Quintana. 2010. Quantification via Probability Estimators. In *2010 IEEE International Conference on Data Mining*, pages 737–742.

Su Lin Blodgett, Lisa Green, and Brendan O'Connor. 2016. Demographic Dialectal Variation in Social Media: A Case Study of African-American English. In *Proceedings of the 2016 Conference on Empirical Methods in Natural Language Processing*, pages 1119–1130, Austin, Texas. Association for Computational Linguistics.

Franck Burlot and François Yvon. 2017. Evaluating the morphological competence of Machine Translation Systems. In *Proceedings of the Second Conference on Machine Translation*, pages 43–55, Copenhagen, Denmark. Association for Computational Linguistics.

Stevie Chancellor, Michael L. Birnbaum, Eric D. Caine, Vincent M. B. Silenzio, and Munmun De Choudhury. 2019. A Taxonomy of Ethical Tensions in Inferring Mental Health States from Social Media. In *Proceedings of the Conference on Fairness, Accountability, and Transparency*, FAT* '19, page 79–88, New York, NY, USA. Association for Computing Machinery.

Ting Chen, Simon Kornblith, Mohammad Norouzi, and Geoffrey Hinton. 2020. A Simple Framework for Contrastive Learning of Visual Representations. In *Proceedings of the 37th International Conference on Machine Learning*, volume 119 of *Proceedings of Machine Learning Research*, pages 1597–1607. PMLR.

Noam Chomsky. 1957. *Syntactic structures*. Mouton.

Holly K Craig and Julie A Washington. 2006. *Malik goes to school: Examining the language skills of African American students from preschool-5th grade*. Psychology Press.

Patricia Cukor-Avila and Ashley Balcazar. 2019. Exploring Grammatical Variation in the Corpus of Regional African American Language. *American Speech*, 94(1):36–53.

Mark Davies. 2016. Corpus del Español: Web/Dialects.

Dorottya Demszky, Devyani Sharma, Jonathan Clark, Vinodkumar Prabhakaran, and Jacob Eisenstein. 2021. Learning to Recognize Dialect Features. In *Proceedings of the 2021 Conference of the North American Chapter of the Association for Computational Linguistics: Human Language Technologies*, pages 2315–2338, Online. Association for Computational Linguistics.

Jacob Devlin, Ming-Wei Chang, Kenton Lee, and Kristina Toutanova. 2019. BERT: Pre-training of Deep Bidirectional Transformers for Language Understanding. In *NAACL-HLT (1)*, pages 4171–4186.

Jacob Eisenstein. 2015. Systematic patterning in phonologically-motivated orthographic variation. *Journal of Sociolinguistics*, 19(2):161–188.

∀, Wilhelmina Nekoto, Vukosi Marivate, Tshinondiwa Matsila, Timi Fasubaa, Taiwo Fagbohungbe, Solomon Oluwole Akinola, Shamsuddeen Muhammad, Salomon Kabongo Kabenamualu, Salomey Osei, Freshia Sackey, Rubungo Andre Niyongabo, Ricky Macharm, Perez Ogayo, Orevaoghene Ahia, Musie Meressa Berhe, Mofetoluwa Adeyemi, Masabata Mokgesi-Selinga, Lawrence Okegbemi, Laura Martinus, Kolawole Tajudeen, Kevin Degila, Kelechi Ogueji, Kathleen Siminyu, Julia Kreutzer, Jason Webster, Jamiil Toure Ali, Jade Abbott, Iroro Orife, Ignatius Ezeani, Idris Abdulkadir Dangana, Herman Kamper, Hady Elsahar, Goodness Duru, Ghollah Kioko, Murhabazi Espoir, Elan van Biljon, Daniel Whitenack, Christopher Onyefuluchi, Chris Chinenye Emezue, Bonaventure F. P. Dossou, Blessing Sibanda, Blessing Bassey, Ayodele Olabiyi, Arshath Ramkilowan, Alp Öktem, Adewale Akinfaderin, and Abdallah Bashir. 2020. Participatory Research for Low-resourced Machine Translation: A Case Study in African Languages. In *Findings of the Association for Computational Linguistics: EMNLP 2020*, pages 2144–2160, Online. Association for Computational Linguistics.

Matt Gardner, Yoav Artzi, Victoria Basmov, Jonathan Berant, Ben Bogin, Sihao Chen, Pradeep Dasigi, Dheeru Dua, Yanai Elazar, Ananth Gottumukkala, Nitish Gupta, Hannaneh Hajishirzi, Gabriel Ilharco, Daniel Khashabi, Kevin Lin, Jiangming Liu, Nelson F. Liu, Phoebe Mulcaire, Qiang Ning, Sameer Singh, Noah A. Smith, Sanjay Subramanian, Reut Tsarfaty, Eric Wallace, Ally Zhang, and Ben Zhou. 2020. Evaluating Models' Local Decision Boundaries via Contrast Sets. In *Findings of the Association for Computational Linguistics: EMNLP 2020*, pages 1307–1323, Online. Association for Computational Linguistics.

Lisa Green. 2017. Beyond Lists of Differences to Accurate Descriptions. In *Data Collection in Sociolinguistics*, pages 281–284. Routledge.

Lisa J Green. 2002. *African American English: A Linguistic Introduction*. Cambridge University Press.

Sidney Greenbaum and Gerald Nelson. 1996. The International Corpus of English (ICE) Project. *World Englishes*, 15(1):3–15.

Jessica A. Grieser. 2019. Investigating Topic-Based Style Shifting in the Classic Sociolinguistic Interview. *American Speech*, 94(1):54–71.

Jack Grieve, Douglas Biber, Eric Friginal, and Tatiana Nekrasova. 2011. *Variation Among Blogs: A Multi-dimensional Analysis*, pages 303–322. Springer Netherlands, Dordrecht.

Kristina Gulordava, Piotr Bojanowski, Edouard Grave, Tal Linzen, and Marco Baroni. 2018. Colorless Green Recurrent Networks Dream Hierarchically. In *Proceedings of the 2018 Conference of the North American Chapter of the Association for Computational Linguistics: Human Language Technologies, Volume 1 (Long Papers)*, pages 1195–1205, New Orleans, Louisiana. Association for Computational Linguistics.

Taylor Jones. 2015. Toward a Description of African American Vernacular English Dialect Regions Using "Black Twitter". *American Speech*, 90(4):403–440.

Tyler Kendall and Charlie Farrington. 2021. The Corpus of Regional African American Language. Eugene, OR: The Online Resources for African American Language Project.

Allison Koenecke, Andrew Nam, Emily Lake, Joe Nudell, Minnie Quartey, Zion Mengesha, Connor Toups, John R. Rickford, Dan Jurafsky, and Sharad Goel. 2020. Racial disparities in automated speech recognition. *Proceedings of the National Academy of Sciences*, 117(14):7684–7689.

Jacob Leon Kröger, Leon Gellrich, Sebastian Pape, Saba Rebecca Brause, and Stefan Ullrich. 2022. Personal information inference from voice recordings: User awareness and privacy concerns. *Proceedings on Privacy Enhancing Technologies*, 2022(1):6–27.

Claudia Lange. 2012. *The Syntax of Spoken Indian English*, volume 45. John Benjamins Publishing.

Manuscript Division Library of Congress. 2001. Born in Slavery: Slave Narratives from the Federal Writers' Project, 1936 to 1938.

Taylor Mahler, Willy Cheung, Micha Elsner, David King, Marie-Catherine de Marneffe, Cory Shain, Symon Stevens-Guille, and Michael White. 2017. Breaking NLP: Using Morphosyntax, Semantics, Pragmatics and World Knowledge to Fool Sentiment Analysis Systems. In *Proceedings of the First Workshop on Building Linguistically Generalizable NLP Systems*, pages 33–39, Copenhagen, Denmark. Association for Computational Linguistics.

Natalie Maynor. 1988. Written Records of Spoken Language: How Reliable Are They. *Methods in Dialectology*, pages 109–20.

Zhengjie Miao, Yuliang Li, Xiaolan Wang, and Wang-Chiew Tan. 2020. *Snippext: Semi-Supervised Opinion Mining with Augmented Data*, page 617–628. Association for Computing Machinery, New York, NY, USA.

Dong Nguyen, A. Seza Doğruöz, Carolyn P. Rosé, and Franciska de Jong. 2016. Computational Sociolinguistics: A Survey. *Comput. Linguist.*, 42(3):537–593.

Jennifer Renn and J. Michael Terry. 2009. Operationalizing Style: Quantifying the Use of Style Shift in the Speech of African American Adolescents. *American Speech*, 84(4):367–390.

Alexis Ross, Tongshuang Wu, Hao Peng, Matthew E. Peters, and Matt Gardner. 2021. Tailor: Generating and Perturbing Text with Semantic Controls. *CoRR*, abs/2107.07150.

Marco Saerens, Patrice Latinne, and Christine Decaestecker. 2002. Adjusting the Outputs of a Classifier to New a Priori Probabilities: A Simple Procedure. *Neural Computation*, 14(1):21–41.

Harrison Santiago, Joshua Martin, Sarah Moeller, and Kevin Tang. 2022. Disambiguation of morphosyntactic features of African American English – the case of habitual be.

Rico Sennrich. 2017. How Grammatical is Character-level Neural Machine Translation? Assessing MT Quality with Contrastive Translation Pairs. In *Proceedings of the 15th Conference of the European Chapter of the Association for Computational Linguistics: Volume 2, Short Papers*, pages 376–382, Valencia, Spain. Association for Computational Linguistics.

Devyani Sharma. 2017. Scalar effects of social networks on language variation. *Language Variation and Change*, 29(3):393–418.

Devyani Sharma. 2018. Style dominance: Attention, audience, and the 'real me'. *Language in Society*, 47(1):1–31.

Noah A. Smith and Jason Eisner. 2005. Contrastive Estimation: Training Log-Linear Models on Unlabeled Data. In *Proceedings of the 43rd Annual Meeting on Association for Computational Linguistics*, ACL '05, page 354–362, USA. Association for Computational Linguistics.

Ieva Staliūnaitė and Ben Bonfil. 2017. Breaking Sentiment Analysis of Movie Reviews. In *Proceedings of the First Workshop on Building Linguistically Generalizable NLP Systems*, pages 61–64, Copenhagen,

Denmark. Association for Computational Linguistics.

Alexandre Veronese, Alessandra Silveira, and Amanda Nunes Lopes Espiñeira Lemos. 2019. Artificial intelligence, Digital Single Market and the proposal of a right to fair and reasonable inferences: a legal issue between ethics and techniques. *UNIO – EU Law Journal*, 5(2):75–91.

C Wilson and V Mihalicek. 2011. *Language Files: Materials for an Introduction to Language and Linguistics*. Columbus: Ohio State University Press.

Walt Wolfram. 1990. Re-Examining Vernacular Black English. *Language*, 66(1):121–133.

A Feature inventories

Level	IndE Feature	Example utterance
Noun phrase	Non-initial existential *there*	library facility was not there
	Focus *itself*	We are feeling tired now itself
	Focus *only*	I like dressing up I told you at the beginning only
Verb phrase	Zero copula	Everybody (is) so worried about the exams
Sentence level	Left dislocation	we elders, we don't have much time to converse
	Resumptive subject pronoun	the father, sometimes he is unemployed
	Resumptive object pronoun	also pickles, we eat it with this jaggery and lot of butter
	Topicalized object (argument)	brothers and sisters you have
	Topicalized non-argument constituent	with your child you have come
	Invariant tag *no/na/isn't it*	both works same hours, isn't it?

Table 2: Features of Indian English used in our study.

Level	Grammatical domain	AAE Feature	Example utterance
Noun phrase	Pronominal case	Zero possessive -*'s*	go over my grandmama('s) house
Verb phrase	Copula deletion	Zero copula	she (is) the folk around here
	Tense marking	Double marked/overregularized	she likeded me the best
	Aspect marking	Habitual *be*	I just be liking the beat
		Resultant *done*	you done lost your mind
	Other verbal markers	*finna*	she's finna have a baby
		come	she come grabbing me on my shirt
		Double modal	he might could really get our minds
	Negation	Negative concord	I ain't doing nothing wrong
		Negative auxiliary inversion	don't nobody know what I had
		Non-inverted negative concord	nobody don't say nothing
		Preverbal negator *ain't*	I ain't doing nothing wrong
Sentence level	Subject-verb agreement	Zero 3rd p sg present tense -*s*	I don't know if it count(s)
		is/was-generalization	they is die hard Laker fans
	Number marking	Zero plural -*s*	about four or five month(s)
	Ditransitive constructions	Double-object construction	I got me my own car
	Interrogative constructions	*Wh*-question	what they was doing?

Table 3: Features of African American English used in our study.

B Approach descriptions

B.1 Proposed approach

A positive example p is defined as $(x_1, x_2, ..., x_n)$ where x_i is a subtoken. For each positive example p:

1. A 3-gram instance t in p is defined as (x_i, x_{i+1}, x_{i+2}). For each 3-gram instance t in p:
   (a) For each $n \in \{2, 3, 4\}$, find the 3 most frequent n-grams from the corpus where, for each n-gram t', the set difference between $set(t)$ and $set(t')$ is at most one subtoken.
   (b) Create perturbed examples by swapping t for t'. These perturbed examples may or may not have the feature.
2. Randomly order the perturbed examples.
3. Manually filter and label the perturbed examples; examples that pass the filter should not have invalid subtoken combinations, positive examples should unambiguously have the feature, and negative examples should unambiguously not have the feature. Examples that pass the filter (positive or negative) may be ungrammatical. Stop after 2 positives and 3 negatives have passed the filter. Including the original positive example p, you should have 3 positives and 3 negatives.

We provide here an example of our approach. For the feature zero copula, we are given $p =$ He on the five dollar. We generate:

Perturbed example
He on the last five
He on the five
on the other five dollar
He on the five hundred dollar
He was on the dollar
on the five dollar
the on five dollar
He and five on the dollar
He was on the five dollar
He on the five dollar bill
He beating on the five dollar
He on the dollar
He on the other dollar
He on five dollar
He the five dollar
He on five dollar bill
was on the five dollar

The manually filtered contrast set looks like:

Example	Label
He on the five dollar	1
He on the last five	1
He on the five	1
on the other five dollar	0
He was on the dollar	0
on the five dollar	0

B.2 Manual generation

Given a positive example p, manually construct a negative example by modifying p so they are (1) semantically-similar MAE versions, and (2) do not have the feature.

B.3 Automatic generation

For each positive example p:

1. Randomly choose n-gram order, where n is some value 0 < n < length(p) - 1.
2. Split positive example into sequential non-overlapping n-grams from left to right. If length of sentence isn't a multiple of n, then the remaining words form an additional m-gram (m < n).
3. Randomly shuffle the list of n-grams.
4. Repeat steps 1-3 until you have three distinct shuffled negative examples per positive example.[7]

B.4 Automatic identification

Randomly choose unlabeled examples from target corpus and label them as the negative examples. Five negatives are chosen per positive example.[8]

C Extended results and figures

Tables 4, 5, and 6 are per-feature results for Indian English features in ICE-India. Tables 7 and 8 are per-feature results for African American English features in CORAAL and FWP. Tables 9, 10, and 11 are standard deviation scores for Indian English features in ICE-India. Figures 4, 5, and 6 are detailed results from replicating prior sociolinguistic work.

[7]Number of negatives per positive was a tuned hyperparameter.

[8]Number of negatives per positive was a tuned hyperparameter.

Feature	ROC-AUC					
	AutoG.	AutoID	MnlG.	AutoID +MnlG.	CGEdit	MnlG. +CGEdit
Non-init. exist. *there*	91.14	90.47	89.88	89.74	95.46	89.03
Focus *itself*	94.08	98.02	98.70	97.58	99.49	99.89
Focus *only*	85.38	97.00	98.94	95.40	96.72	99.02
Zero copula	53.28	61.82	73.75	67.77	73.79	75.61
Left dislocation	64.17	70.18	93.13	69.32	89.92	93.14
Res. subject pronoun	72.81	70.03	93.60	67.92	88.32	89.94
Res. object pronoun	67.49	70.46	86.87	78.24	86.44	88.93
Topic. object (arg.)	63.20	59.17	76.72	54.28	72.08	81.30
Topic. non-arg. const.	44.90	55.48	69.24	55.55	59.99	79.54
Invar. tag *no/na/isn't it*	52.96	76.37	87.46	87.55	86.95	91.24
Macro average	68.94	74.90	86.83	76.34	84.92	88.76

Table 4: ROC-AUC results on ICE-India, averaged over 3 runs.

Feature	AP					
	AutoG.	AutoID	MnlG.	AutoID +MnlG.	CGEdit	MnlG. +CGEdit
Non-init. exist. *there*	46.56	41.32	53.16	51.84	61.11	59.56
Focus *itself*	39.99	40.16	74.76	72.76	78.12	75.14
Focus *only*	24.23	32.74	40.04	28.12	41.10	44.31
Zero copula	01.78	04.96	02.05	04.19	03.88	02.95
Left dislocation	02.78	05.70	25.78	09.47	23.07	26.63
Res. subject pronoun	03.68	03.57	21.72	07.55	20.64	20.50
Res. object pronoun	00.24	01.58	02.47	00.93	02.96	05.66
Topic. object (arg.)	02.04	15.95	06.99	02.13	06.00	10.16
Topic. non-arg. const.	01.11	02.53	03.78	02.26	02.65	06.10
Invar. tag *no/na/isn't it*	03.89	04.96	26.95	20.26	37.26	42.18
Macro average	12.63	15.24	25.77	19.95	27.48	29.32

Table 5: AP results on ICE-India, averaged over 3 runs.

Feature	Prec@100					
	AutoG.	AutoID	MnlG.	AutoID +MnlG.	CGEdit	MnlG. +CGEdit
Non-init. exist. *there*	78.33	74.00	86.00	82.00	84.33	87.00
Focus *itself*	15.67	18.67	28.00	25.00	28.00	28.00
Focus *only*	34.33	41.33	48.33	39.67	45.00	48.33
Zero copula	03.33	01.67	03.33	05.00	03.00	05.33
Left dislocation	08.33	18.33	46.33	27.00	42.67	42.00
Res. subject pronoun	09.67	13.67	39.00	24.67	36.00	31.67
Res. object pronoun	00.00	01.00	03.67	01.67	04.67	08.33
Topic. object (arg.)	05.67	03.00	15.00	06.67	12.33	19.33
Topic. non-arg. const.	01.33	01.00	07.33	06.33	07.00	13.67
Invar. tag *no/na/isn't it*	12.67	06.00	39.33	25.00	62.00	73.00
Macro average	16.93	17.87	31.63	24.30	32.50	35.67

Table 6: Prec@100 results on ICE-India, averaged over 3 runs.Prec@100 results on CORAAL. Note that if there are less than 100 instances of a certain feature (e.g. *finna* occurs only 35 times in this dataset, confirmed via keyword search), then its Prec@100 score will have an upper bound of less than 1.

Feature	Prec@100 MNLG.	CGEDIT	MNLG. +CGEDIT
Zero possessive -*'s*	030.0	071.0	088.0
Zero copula	089.0	100. 0	100.0
Double marked	024.0	031.0	045.0
Habitual *be*	100.0	100.0	100.0
Resultant *done*	089.0	097.0	097.0
finna	035.0	035.0	035.0
come	011.0	016.0	015.0
Double modal	014.0	014.0	013.0
Negative concord	100.0	096.0	077.0
Neg. auxiliary inversion	078.0	096.0	089.0
Non-inverted neg. concord	009.0	010.0	012.0
Preverbal negator *ain't*	100.0	100.0	100.0
Zero 3rd p sg pres. tense -*s*	096.0	100.0	098.0
is/was-generalization	063.0	100.0	100.0
Zero plural -*s*	017.0	062.0	059.0
Double-object construction	050.0	030.0	018.0
Wh-question	079.0	088.0	058.0
Macro average	057.9	067.4	064.9

Table 7: Prec@100 results on CORAAL. Note that if there are less than 100 instances of a certain feature (e.g. *finna* occurs only 35 times in this dataset, confirmed via keyword search), then its Prec@100 score will have an upper bound of less than 1.

Feature	Prec@100 MNLG.	CGEDIT	MNLG. +CGEDIT
Zero possessive -*'s*	011.0	042.0	026.0
Zero copula	097.0	099.0	100.0
Double marked	053.0	049.0	095.0
Habitual *be*	078.0	099.0	097.0
Resultant *done*	093.0	100.0	100.0
finna	000.0	000.0	000.0
come	001.0	050.0	082.0
Double modal	004.0	005.0	004.0
Negative concord	100.0	100.0	100.0
Neg. auxiliary inversion	093.0	100.0	100.0
Non-inverted neg. concord	015.0	024.0	056.0
Preverbal negator *ain't*	100.0	100.0	100.0
Zero 3rd p sg pres. tense -*s*	100.0	100.0	100.0
is/was-generalization	100.0	100.0	100.0
Zero plural -*s*	024.0	070.0	096.0
Double-object construction	036.0	028.0	020.0
Wh-question	093.0	090.0	088.0
Macro average	058.7	068.0	074.4

Table 8: Prec@100 results on FWP. Note that if there are less than 100 instances of a certain feature (e.g. *finna* occurs 0 times in this dataset, confirmed via keyword search), then its Prec@100 score will have an upper bound of less than 1.

Feature	ROC-AUC Standard Deviation					
	AutoG.	AutoID	MnlG.	AutoID +MnlG.	CGEdit	MnlG. +CGEdit
Non-init. exist. *there*	03.29	00.69	00.65	07.39	01.89	08.42
Focus *itself*	03.38	00.54	00.42	00.45	00.47	00.03
Focus *only*	06.40	01.59	00.66	01.25	02.74	00.48
Zero copula	04.63	03.80	07.95	04.71	06.87	01.04
Left dislocation	07.90	01.83	01.24	16.00	01.62	00.78
Res. subject pronoun	04.62	07.10	00.39	17.13	04.77	05.24
Res. object pronoun	04.73	06.15	05.66	07.79	01.77	00.70
Topic. object (arg.)	06.20	02.88	10.93	06.49	04.89	05.39
Topic. non-arg. const.	03.25	05.52	03.87	01.79	05.57	03.31
Invar. tag *no/na/isn't it*	07.64	04.35	03.04	01.59	10.77	04.97
Macro average	05.20	03.45	03.48	06.46	04.14	03.04

Table 9: Standard deviation of ROC-AUC results on ICE-India over 3 runs.

Feature	AP Standard Deviation					
	AutoG.	AutoID	MnlG.	AutoID +MnlG.	CGEdit	MnlG. +CGEdit
Non-init. exist. *there*	09.52	03.07	04.32	15.13	09.13	08.09
Focus *itself*	09.87	11.30	03.44	08.26	04.30	08.19
Focus *only*	08.36	02.62	05.68	08.01	04.74	00.43
Zero copula	01.79	05.45	01.22	02.07	01.50	01.36
Left dislocation	00.80	01.31	04.90	05.84	01.36	00.78
Res. subject pronoun	00.70	03.12	07.30	05.54	08.82	04.91
Res. object pronoun	00.07	01.77	00.72	00.89	00.65	01.83
Topic. object (arg.)	01.29	25.05	02.46	00.57	01.31	01.18
Topic. non-arg. const.	00.13	01.93	00.99	00.96	00.93	00.39
Invar. tag *no/na/isn't it*	00.73	03.02	13.96	07.02	25.90	16.98
Macro average	03.33	05.86	04.50	05.43	05.86	04.41

Table 10: Standard deviation of AP results on ICE-India over 3 runs.

Feature	Prec@100 Standard Deviation					
	AutoG.	AutoID	MnlG.	AutoID +MnlG.	CGEdit	MnlG. +CGEdit
Non-init. exist. *there*	08.02	07.00	04.00	12.90	04.16	03.61
Focus *itself*	03.51	04.04	00.00	31.19	00.00	00.00
Focus *only*	06.03	04.16	06.43	07.13	05.57	05.51
Zero copula	01.15	01.53	02.08	01.30	03.00	01.53
Left dislocation	04.04	06.66	05.20	34.27	05.51	02.65
Res. subject pronoun	04.51	03.21	14.73	21.81	17.69	07.09
Res. object pronoun	00.00	00.00	01.15	02.89	00.58	02.52
Topic. object (arg.)	03.79	02.65	05.20	06.48	02.31	03.51
Topic. non-arg. const.	00.58	00.00	03.21	07.57	03.00	03.79
Invar. tag *no/na/isn't it*	04.16	04.36	16.20	38.91	25.51	17.09
Macro average	03.58	03.36	06.15	16.45	06.73	04.73

Table 11: Standard deviation of Prec@100 results on ICE-India over 3 runs.

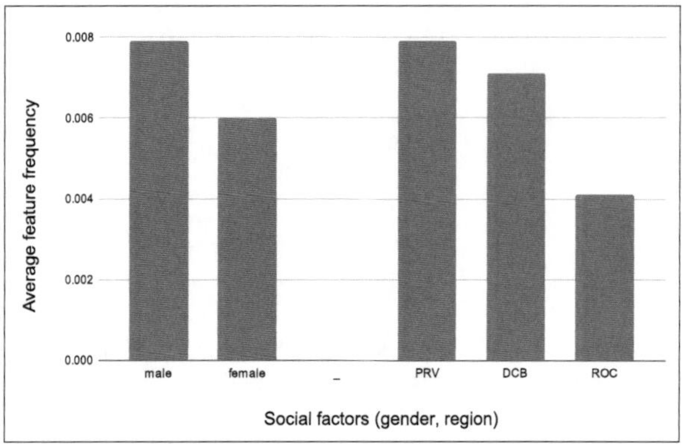

Figure 4: Confirming results from Koenecke et al. (2020). Examined 17 features over entire DCB, PRV, and ROC subcorpora. We find higher feature frequencies among male speakers than female speakers; and highest feature frequency in Princeville, followed by DC, and then Rochester.

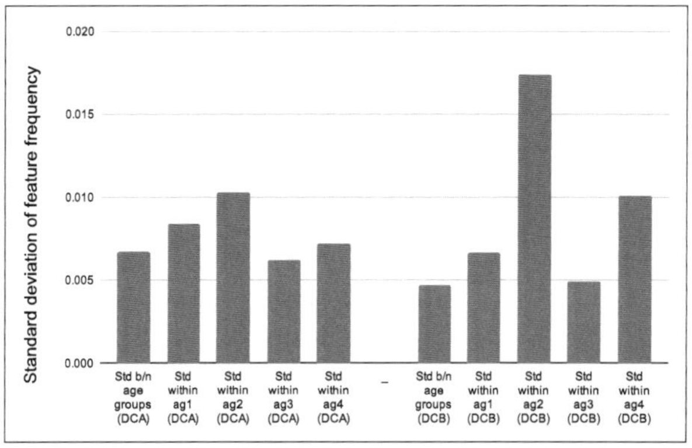

Figure 5: Confirming results from Cukor-Avila and Balcazar (2019). Examined 3 features over files specified in their study from DCA and DCB subcorpora. Ag1 corresponds to ages less than 20, ag2 corresponds to ages 20-29, ag3 corresponds to 30-50, and ag4 corresponds to 50+. We find that standard deviation between speakers in an age group is equal to or larger than standard deviation between age groups.

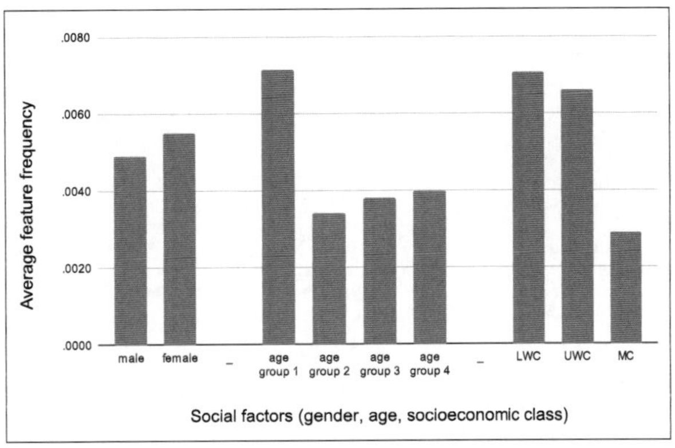

Figure 6: Confirming results from Grieser (2019). Examined 14 features over files specified in their study from DCA subcorpus. Age group 1 corresponds to ages less than 20, age group 2 corresponds to ages 20-29, age group 3 corresponds to 30-50, and age group 4 corresponds to 50+; the socioeconomic classes, from left to right, are Lower Working Class, Upper Working Class, and Middle Class. We find that age and socioeconomic status are negatively correlated with feature use. We find that men have a slightly lower average feature frequency; however, when looking at all of CORAAL for all of our features, we confirm that men have a higher average feature frequency. This is perhaps an example of how small sample size can skew results.

Machine Translation Between High-resource Languages in a Language Documentation Setting

Katharina Kann and **Abteen Ebrahimi** and **Kristine Stenzel** and **Alexis Palmer**
University of Colorado Boulder
first.last@colorado.edu

Abstract

Language documentation encompasses translation, typically into the dominant high-resource language in the region where the target language is spoken. To make data accessible to a broader audience, additional translation into other high-resource languages might be needed. Working within a project documenting Kotiria, we explore the extent to which state-of-the-art machine translation (MT) systems can support this second translation – in our case from Portuguese to English. This translation task is challenging for multiple reasons: (1) the data is out-of-domain with respect to the MT system's training data, (2) much of the data is conversational, (3) existing translations include non-standard and uncommon expressions, often reflecting properties of the documented language, and (4) the data includes borrowings from other regional languages. Despite these challenges, existing MT systems perform at a usable level, though there is still room for improvement. We then conduct a qualitative analysis and suggest ways to improve MT between high-resource languages in a language documentation setting.

1 Introduction

We report on our investigations of whether and how existing machine translation (MT) systems can support the work of documenting and describing endangered languages. Rather than targeting low-resource MT, we look at translating between high-resource languages, aiming to save time for the language experts and language community members working on the language documentation project.

Specifically, we are working with a linguist documenting Kotiria (also known as *Wanano*), an East Tukano language spoken in the Brazil-Colombia borderlands in northwestern Amazonia. Documentation and description of Kotiria on the Brazilian side of the border has been ongoing since 2000, resulting in numerous publications, including a Reference Grammar (Stenzel, 2013), and a documentary archive of primarily monologic language data (approx. 10 hours of mythical, historical, and personal narratives, public addresses, and instructional speech). A second documentation project focusing on language use and interaction in daily life resulted in a much larger corpus – approximately 60 hours – of primarily conversational data. Both projects were carried out within the participatory research paradigm (Stenzel, 2014), with indigenous speakers involved in both recording and annotation of data in ELAN,[1] including translation of the indigenous language data into Portuguese.

Further grammatical analysis and annotation of these documentary materials, including translation from Portuguese into English, is ongoing but proceeds slowly. Researchers of endangered languages worldwide generally work alone or at best in small teams to deal with enormous amounts of data, further underscoring the gap between technological advances that facilitate production of large, high quality documentary corpora and researchers' ability to single-handedly process the resulting materials. The Kotiria case is no different, and even basic tasks, such as adding English translations to the two existing corpora, extend over years.

The corpus from the more recent Kotiria language documentation project presents additional challenges. First, language use in conversation is by its very nature more complex to annotate and analyze than monologic speech because it is rife with features such as reductions, cut-offs, overlaps, intonational contours, and other details of production, as well as grammatical structures whose meaning can only be understood in sequential context (Hepburn and Bolden, 2013). Additionally, due to the multilingual nature of social life in the region where Kotiria is spoken (Stenzel, 2005; Stenzel and Williams, 2021), recordings contain numerous instances of speech in other indigenous languages, such as Tukano. Though extremely rich, such data constitutes a lifetime (or perhaps several lifetimes)

[1] https://archive.mpi.nl/tla/elan

Proceedings of the first workshop on NLP applications to field linguistics, pages 26–33
July 5–10, 2020. ©2020 Association for Computational Linguistics
https://doi.org/10.26615/978-954-452-056-4_003

of processing work for a lone-wolf researcher.

Automatic translation – or *machine translation (MT)* – has made tremendous progress over the last few years (Sutskever et al., 2014; Bahdanau et al., 2014; Vaswani et al., 2017), and MT systems are used more and more in everyday life, e.g., in browser extensions, smartphone apps, or as a first translation pass in software for professional (human) translators. Initial translations in a language documentation project are often made into the dominant high-resource language in the documented language's region (Portuguese for Kotiria). As MT between high-resource languages is typically of high quality (Akhbardeh et al., 2021), we investigate if MT systems can assist with producing additional translations between the region's dominant high-resource language (Portuguese) and English, which can help make the created resources accessible to a broader community. Our goal is to produce first-pass translations automatically, such that the language experts in the language documentation project need not devote years to the process, but rather can do post-correction of the first-pass translations. This should yield significant time savings (Toral et al., 2018), freeing up the experts to work on other aspects of the project.

Importantly, such a translation in a documentation context constitutes multiple challenges not present in general MT: (1) the sentences that need to be translated are out-of-domain with respect to the system's training data, (2) the data is conversational, (3) the source-side data contains nonstandard and uncommon expressions, often reflecting properties of the documented language, and (4) the text includes borrowings from other regional languages. While those challenges could be minimized by training on in-domain data from the concrete translation task, such data is generally either not available or too small for effective finetuning.

First, we employ 3 state-of-the-art MT systems to translate Portuguese sentences for which we have gold-standard translations into English. We evaluate the results both manually and with automatic metrics and find that Google Translate performs best. Second, we analyse the outputs of Google Translate, exploring what types of examples it fails and succeeds on. We observe that the conversational nature of the Kotiria data and particular properties of Kotiria-to-Portuguese translations cause many errors. We end by discussing how to improve MT for language documentation data.

2 Related Work

NLP for Language Documentation One goal of language documentation is to create permanent records of the linguistic and cultural practices of understudied speech communities and combat loss of linguistic diversity. It encompasses the audio and video recording of speech as well as the transcription, translation, and analysis of the recordings. This process is costly in terms of time and money, and, besides MT into additional high-resource languages, NLP has the potential to aid documentation via automatic speech recognition (Adams et al., 2018; Prud'hommeaux et al., 2021; Shi et al., 2021; Liu et al., 2022), improve access to legacy materials through OCR (Rijhwani et al., 2020), enrich text data with part-of-speech tags (Eskander et al., 2020) or word boundaries (Okabe et al., 2022) to eventually obtain interlinear glossed text, or to support the analysis of a language's morphology (Jin et al., 2020; Moeller et al., 2020), *inter alia*.

MT of Out-of-Domain Data Our setting requires MT models to generalize to out-of-domain data: available translations are too few for training or finetuning, and, in other language documentation settings, no translations into additional high-resource languages might be available at all. However, MT systems often struggle to perform well on data they have not been trained on – e.g., systems trained on 2019 news do not perform well on 2020 news, due to a topic shift towards the coronavirus (Anastasopoulos et al., 2020). Domain adaptation (DA), which has been studied extensively (Yang et al., 2018; Chu et al., 2018; Adams et al., 2022), though not in the context of a language documentation workflow, can yield improvements. Techniques include finetuning (Luong and Manning, 2015; Freitag and Al-Onaizan, 2016) or backtranslation (Sennrich et al., 2016). For surveys on DA for MT, we refer readers to Chu and Wang (2018); Saunders (2021). We investigate how well general state-of-the-art MT systems translate between high-resource languages in a language documentation setting. In future work, we will take inspiration from research on DA and investigate how to build better systems for our use case.

3 Experimental Setup

3.1 Data

Our dataset draws from the two Kotiria documentation projects described in Section 1, i.e., we have a

Meaning	5	Exactly the same meaning as gold (except for parts that appear in Portuguese but not in gold)
	4	About the same meaning as gold; maybe minor differences (like singular/plural or similar)
	3	Meaning can maybe be guessed but is not clear from the translation or something is misleading
	2	The meaning is different/partially misleading and only a few words are in common with gold
	1	The meaning of this translation has absolutely nothing to do with gold or is misleading
Rel. Fluency	5	Completely fluent in English; maybe more fluent than reference translation
	4	As fluent as reference translation or minor grammatical error that does not affect understanding
	3	Understandable, but not completely fluent
	2	Not a fluent sentence, understandable with lots of effort
	1	Not understandable because of lack of fluency

Table 1: The annotation instructions we provide to our annotators to assess translation quality in terms of *meaning* and *relative fluency*.

mix of monologic and conversational texts. Across the two projects, we have 2267 sentences with reference English translations, which we divide evenly into development and test sets. We report results on the development set to reserve the test set for future research on MT systems for this setting.[2]

3.2 MT Systems

M2M-100 M2M-100 (Fan et al., 2021) is a model trained to handle many-to-many translation between 100 languages. It is a transformer encoder–decoder, and for this work we use the version with 418M parameters. M2M-100 uses SentencePiece (Kudo and Richardson, 2018) tokenization and is trained on mined parallel data, extending prior work (El-Kishky et al., 2020; Schwenk et al., 2021). The model is not trained on data from all possible pairs – rather, languages are grouped, and only within-group language pairs are used for training. Bridge languages are chosen for each language group and trained against other bridge languages. In addition, all languages are trained against English. The training set has 7.5 billion examples.

mBART50 mBART (Liu et al., 2020) is a sequence-to-sequence autoencoder, pretrained with a denoising objective. The model is pretrained on 25 languages, with the goal of recovering the original input after it has been corrupted with a noise function, which involves sentence re-ordering and span masking. It is then finetuned for translation using parallel data. However, since Portuguese is not included in the original set of languages, for this work we use mBART50 (Tang et al., 2021), which builds upon the original mBART model and extends the number of languages from 25 to 50. We use the version trained with multilingual finetuning, allowing for many-to-many translation.

Google Translate We also compare to a state-of-the-art commercial MT system: Google Translate.[3] For our experiments we use Googletrans,[4] a python library accessing the Google Translate Ajax API.

3.3 Automatic Metrics

We use two automatic metrics for evaluation, which we calculate using SacreBLEU (Post, 2018).

BLEU First, we evaluate our outputs with BLEU (Papineni et al., 2002), the standard metric for MT. BLEU measures word overlap between the translation and the reference. We use SacreBLEU's default settings and tokenization.

ChrF We further compute ChrF (Popović, 2015). In contrast to BLEU, this metric measures the *character* overlap between a translation and a reference.

3.4 Human Evaluation

In addition to employing automatic metrics we also perform a manual/human evaluation of translations for a subset of 100 randomly sampled sentences from the development set. We show annotators the Portuguese source sentence, the English reference, and the system output and ask for an assessment along two axes: meaning (*does the translation's meaning correspond to the reference?*) and (relative) fluency (*is it as grammatical as the reference?*). Both meaning and fluency are assessed using a Likert scale from 1 to 5, with higher numbers indicating better quality. We give annotators the option to skip examples whose fluency and meaning they feel unable to judge, e.g., "Uhh". Each translation is rated by two annotators, and reported scores are averages over annotators. Table 1 shows the complete instructions given to annotators.

[2]Our data is publicly available at `https://nala-cub.github.io/resources`.

[3]`https://translate.google.com`

[4]`https://py-googletrans.readthedocs.io/`

System	BLEU	ChrF
Google Translate	**19.96**	**42.83**
mBART	9.40	31.39
M2M-100	10.25	30.50

Table 2: Automatic evaluation: BLEU and ChrF for all systems on the development set. Best scores in bold.

System	Meaning	Fluency
Google Translate	**3.82**	**4.07**
mBART	2.57	4.04
M2M-100	3.07	3.72

Table 3: Manual evaluation: meaning and fluency of all systems on 100 sentences from the development set. Scores are averaged over annotators. Best scores in bold.

4 Results and Discussion

4.1 Translation Performance

Automatic Evaluation Table 2 displays the performance of all systems on the development set according to automatic metrics. The best system is Google Translate with a BLEU (resp. ChrF) score of 19.96 (resp. 42.83). The other two systems obtain considerably lower and, surprisingly, quite similar scores: mBART achieves a BLEU and ChrF of 9.40 and, respectively, 31.39, while M2M-100's scores are 10.25 and 30.50.

In absolute terms, the score of Google Translate, the best system in our experiments, is reasonable, but not as good as for general in-domain MT, where BLEU scores higher than 40.00 were reported by Google already in 2017 (Johnson et al., 2017).

Human Evaluation Table 3 shows *meaning* (i.e., how well the translation represents the meaning of the gold translation) and *fluency* scores (i.e., how grammatical the sentence is, given the reference translation). They range from 2.57 to 3.82 for meaning and from 3.72 to 4.07 for fluency. As both scores are on a scale from 1 to 5 with higher being better, all systems perform reasonably well on our task. Thus, our first and main conclusion is that *MT systems can indeed help with language documentation*; specifically with translating from the dominant high-resource language in the region of the documented language into another high-resource language. However, *there is room for improvement.*

Comparing the 3 systems we get a picture similar to the one we get with automatic metrics: Google Translate performs best for both meaning and fluency. Surprisingly, mBART has with 4.04 a high fluency score, which nearly matches that of Google Translate, but a comparatively low meaning score with 2.57. M2M-100 is with 3.07 between the other two systems with regards to meaning, but lags behind the other two as far as fluency is concerned.

Comparing meaning with fluency scores, we observe that systems are similar with respect to the latter (max. delta: 0.35), but vary considerably for the former (max. delta: 1.25). This shows that all systems have been trained on enough English data to produce grammatical sentences. However, generating text that represents the meaning of the Portuguese sentence is more challenging.

4.2 Qualitative Analysis

We continue our analysis to investigate particular weaknesses and some unexpected strengths of MT by investigating the translations produced by Google Translate, the best performing system, according to both automatic and manual evaluations. We focus on issues relevant for data from a language documentation context.

Conversational/Dialog Speech Many fluency errors we see in the MT output can be at least partially attributed to the conversational nature of the original text. For example:

(1) *é, jogar, amanha vamos quebrar com chute*
(Ref) yeah, thrown away, and tomorrow we can kick them in
(GT) yeah, play, tomorrow we're going to break with kick

The utterance in (1) makes sense in its discourse context, with confirmation that an unspecified something has been thrown away: *jogar* means both "play" and "throw" and is used here as a shortened form of *jogar fora* ("throw out/away"). It is followed by a clause with a pronominal object. Absent that context, though, the MT system selects the wrong meaning, supplies no referents, and treats the verbs as infinitives. The result is a nearly incoherent English translation.

Transfer from Kotiria Some of the most interesting errors stem from L1 transfer, as nearly all of the Portuguese translations were written by speakers of Kotiria who had later learned Portuguese as one of their additional languages. In some translations, grammatical properties of Kotiria are transferred into Portuguese, resulting in non-standard forms: e.g., serial verb constructions, in which multiple roots occur contiguously to form a single verb stem, are common in Kotiria but not in Portuguese. In (2), the Kotiria serialized verb construction indicating associated motion is rendered as a sequence of separately inflected verbs, resulting in understandable but odd-sounding Portuguese. Some differences reflect the different morphological inventories of the languages: Portuguese uses a range of different locative markers (indicating different spatial configurations, such as *in*, *on*, or *to*), but Kotiria has a single locative marker subsuming all of these functions. In cases like (3), we see *em* ("in") used as a generic locative marker rather than the context-appropriate *a* ("to") in Portuguese.

(2) *levaram arrastando e que ele estava sentindo mal (tristeza, raivoso)*
(Ref) they dragged him off and he was full of regret
(GT) led dragging and that he was feeling bad (sadness, angry)

(3) *em são gabriel?*
(Ref) to São Gabriel?
(GT) in san gabriel?

Borrowings Another class of translation errors occurs when lexical borrowings from other regional languages appear in the Portuguese text. These are often not translated into English by the MT system.

Unexpected Strengths The translations found in our data often include clarifications/explanations (as seen in (2)) or reduced forms ((4), in which *pra* is a non-standard reduced form of *para*). Google Translate handles these issues surprisingly well.

(4) *pra bateria nao mexer*
(Ref) So the battery won't move again
(GT) so the battery doesn't move

4.3 How to MT for Language Documentation

Here, we investigate how general state-of-the-art models perform in a language documentation context. However, while existing MT models work surprisingly well for language documentation purposes, we believe that model adaptation to this specific domain (cf. Section 2) could further improve performance: English translations from documentation corpora of other languages could familiarize the model with conversational English and recurrent themes (e.g., *travel*, *food* or *ceremonies*). The more linguistically similar the documented languages are and the more topic overlap of collected text there is, the more this should help.

Another option – potentially combinable with the first one – would be a multilingual model that is trained (also) on parallel data between the documented language and the first high-resource language. This could teach the model about word choices and expressions, which, later on, would be beneficial for their translation into English.

Finally, the error types pointed out in Section 4.2 are frequent in our corpus, suggesting that MT models would benefit from incorporating explicitly-specified prior knowledge about key structural properties of the language being documented.

5 Conclusion

Using data from the documentation of Kotiria, we investigated how general state-of-the-art MT systems perform when translating from Portuguese to English in a language documentation setting. We found that, among 3 systems, Google Translate performs best and at a level that makes it a promising option for documentary linguists. We then performed a qualitative analysis of Google Translate and observed a number of systematic error patterns directly linked to properties of our language documentation project. Finally, we suggested multiple ways to improve systems for this setting, including model adaptation, targeted multilinguality, and the incorporation of linguistic features.

Acknowledgments

We would like to thank the Kotiria community for their permission to share data from their documentary corpora. We moreover acknowledge the invaluable work on transcription and translation by indigenous research team member Auxiliadora Ferreira Figueiredo. Stenzel's early research on Kotiria received funding through National Science Foundation dissertation (2002- 2004) and Endangered Languages Documentation Program MPD-155 (2007-2011) grants. Recent documentation and analysis were supported by the National Science Foundation under Grant No. BCS-1664348 (2017-2020) and the National Endowment for the Humanities fellowship FN-271117-20 (2020-2021). Any views, findings, conclusions, or recommendations expressed in this article do not necessarily reflect those of the National Endowment for the Humanities and the National Science Foundation.

References

Oliver Adams, Trevor Cohn, Graham Neubig, Hilaria Cruz, Steven Bird, and Alexis Michaud. 2018. Evaluation phonemic transcription of low-resource tonal languages for language documentation. In *Proceedings of the Eleventh International Conference on Language Resources and Evaluation (LREC 2018)*, Miyazaki, Japan. European Language Resources Association (ELRA).

Virginia Adams, Sandeep Subramanian, Mike Chrzanowski, Oleksii Hrinchuk, and Oleksii Kuchaiev. 2022. Finding the right recipe for low resource domain adaptation in neural machine translation. *arXiv preprint arXiv:2206.01137*.

Farhad Akhbardeh, Arkady Arkhangorodsky, Magdalena Biesialska, Ondřej Bojar, Rajen Chatterjee, Vishrav Chaudhary, Marta R. Costa-jussa, Cristina España-Bonet, Angela Fan, Christian Federmann, Markus Freitag, Yvette Graham, Roman Grundkiewicz, Barry Haddow, Leonie Harter, Kenneth Heafield, Christopher Homan, Matthias Huck, Kwabena Amponsah-Kaakyire, Jungo Kasai, Daniel Khashabi, Kevin Knight, Tom Kocmi, Philipp Koehn, Nicholas Lourie, Christof Monz, Makoto Morishita, Masaaki Nagata, Ajay Nagesh, Toshiaki Nakazawa, Matteo Negri, Santanu Pal, Allahsera Auguste Tapo, Marco Turchi, Valentin Vydrin, and Marcos Zampieri. 2021. Findings of the 2021 conference on machine translation (WMT21). In *Proceedings of the Sixth Conference on Machine Translation*, pages 1–88, Online. Association for Computational Linguistics.

Antonios Anastasopoulos, Alessandro Cattelan, Zi-Yi Dou, Marcello Federico, Christian Federmann, Dmitriy Genzel, Franscisco Guzmán, Junjie Hu, Macduff Hughes, Philipp Koehn, Rosie Lazar, Will Lewis, Graham Neubig, Mengmeng Niu, Alp Öktem, Eric Paquin, Grace Tang, and Sylwia Tur. 2020. TICO-19: the translation initiative for COvid-19. In *Proceedings of the 1st Workshop on NLP for COVID-19 (Part 2) at EMNLP 2020*, Online. Association for Computational Linguistics.

Dzmitry Bahdanau, Kyunghyun Cho, and Yoshua Bengio. 2014. Neural machine translation by jointly learning to align and translate. *arXiv preprint arXiv:1409.0473*.

Chenhui Chu, Raj Dabre, and Sadao Kurohashi. 2018. A comprehensive empirical comparison of domain adaptation methods for neural machine translation. *Journal of Information Processing*, 26:529–538.

Chenhui Chu and Rui Wang. 2018. A survey of domain adaptation for neural machine translation. In *Proceedings of the 27th International Conference on Computational Linguistics*, pages 1304–1319, Santa Fe, New Mexico, USA. Association for Computational Linguistics.

Ahmed El-Kishky, Vishrav Chaudhary, Francisco Guzmán, and Philipp Koehn. 2020. CCAligned: A massive collection of cross-lingual web-document pairs. In *Proceedings of the 2020 Conference on Empirical Methods in Natural Language Processing (EMNLP)*, pages 5960–5969, Online. Association for Computational Linguistics.

Ramy Eskander, Smaranda Muresan, and Michael Collins. 2020. Unsupervised cross-lingual part-of-speech tagging for truly low-resource scenarios. In *Proceedings of the 2020 Conference on Empirical Methods in Natural Language Processing (EMNLP)*, pages 4820–4831, Online. Association for Computational Linguistics.

Angela Fan, Shruti Bhosale, Holger Schwenk, Zhiyi Ma, Ahmed El-Kishky, Siddharth Goyal, Mandeep Baines, Onur Çelebi, Guillaume Wenzek, Vishrav Chaudhary, Naman Goyal, Tom Birch, Vitaliy Liptchinsky, Sergey Edunov, Edouard Grave, Michael Auli, and Armand Joulin. 2021. Beyond english-centric multilingual machine translation. *J. Mach. Learn. Res.*, 22:107:1–107:48.

Markus Freitag and Yaser Al-Onaizan. 2016. Fast domain adaptation for neural machine translation. *arXiv preprint arXiv:1612.06897*.

Alexa Hepburn and Galina B. Bolden. 2013. The conversation analytic approach to transcription. In Jack Sidnell and Tanya Stivers, editors, *The Handbook of Conversation Analysis*, pages 57–76. Blackwell.

Huiming Jin, Liwei Cai, Yihui Peng, Chen Xia, Arya McCarthy, and Katharina Kann. 2020. Unsupervised morphological paradigm completion. In *Proceedings of the 58th Annual Meeting of the Association for Computational Linguistics*, pages 6696–6707, Online. Association for Computational Linguistics.

Melvin Johnson, Mike Schuster, Quoc V. Le, Maxim Krikun, Yonghui Wu, Zhifeng Chen, Nikhil Thorat, Fernanda Viégas, Martin Wattenberg, Greg Corrado, Macduff Hughes, and Jeffrey Dean. 2017. Google's multilingual neural machine translation system: Enabling zero-shot translation. *Transactions of the Association for Computational Linguistics*, 5:339–351.

Taku Kudo and John Richardson. 2018. SentencePiece: A simple and language independent subword tokenizer and detokenizer for neural text processing. In *Proceedings of the 2018 Conference on Empirical Methods in Natural Language Processing: System Demonstrations*, pages 66–71, Brussels, Belgium. Association for Computational Linguistics.

Yinhan Liu, Jiatao Gu, Naman Goyal, Xian Li, Sergey Edunov, Marjan Ghazvininejad, Mike Lewis, and Luke Zettlemoyer. 2020. Multilingual denoising pre-training for neural machine translation. *Transactions of the Association for Computational Linguistics*, 8:726–742.

Zoey Liu, Justin Spence, and Emily Tucker Prud'hommeaux. 2022. Enhancing documentation of Hupa with automatic speech recognition. In *Proceedings of the Fifth Workshop on the Use of Computational Methods in the Study of Endangered Languages*, pages 187–192, Dublin, Ireland. Association for Computational Linguistics.

Minh-Thang Luong and Christopher Manning. 2015. Stanford neural machine translation systems for spoken language domains. In *Proceedings of the 12th International Workshop on Spoken Language Translation: Evaluation Campaign*, pages 76–79, Da Nang, Vietnam.

Sarah Moeller, Ling Liu, Changbing Yang, Katharina Kann, and Mans Hulden. 2020. IGT2P: From interlinear glossed texts to paradigms. In *Proceedings of the 2020 Conference on Empirical Methods in Natural Language Processing (EMNLP)*, pages 5251–5262, Online. Association for Computational Linguistics.

Shu Okabe, Laurent Besacier, and François Yvon. 2022. Weakly supervised word segmentation for computational language documentation. In *Proceedings of the 60th Annual Meeting of the Association for Computational Linguistics (Volume 1: Long Papers)*, pages 7385–7398, Dublin, Ireland. Association for Computational Linguistics.

Kishore Papineni, Salim Roukos, Todd Ward, and Wei-Jing Zhu. 2002. Bleu: a Method for Automatic Evaluation of Machine Translation. In *Proceedings of the 40th Annual Meeting of the Association for Computational Linguistics*, pages 311–318, Philadelphia, Pennsylvania, USA. Association for Computational Linguistics.

Maja Popović. 2015. chrF: character n-gram F-score for automatic MT evaluation. In *Proceedings of the Tenth Workshop on Statistical Machine Translation*, pages 392–395, Lisbon, Portugal. Association for Computational Linguistics.

Matt Post. 2018. A call for clarity in reporting BLEU scores. In *Proceedings of the Third Conference on Machine Translation: Research Papers*, pages 186–191, Belgium, Brussels. Association for Computational Linguistics.

Emily Prud'hommeaux, Robbie Jimerson, Richard Hatcher, and Karin Michelson. 2021. Automatic speech recognition for supporting endangered language documentation. *Language Documentation & Conservation*, 15:491–513.

Shruti Rijhwani, Antonios Anastasopoulos, and Graham Neubig. 2020. OCR Post Correction for Endangered Language Texts. In *Proceedings of the 2020 Conference on Empirical Methods in Natural Language Processing (EMNLP)*, pages 5931–5942, Online. Association for Computational Linguistics.

Danielle Saunders. 2021. Domain adaptation and multi-domain adaptation for neural machine translation: A survey. *arXiv preprint arXiv:2104.06951*.

Holger Schwenk, Guillaume Wenzek, Sergey Edunov, Edouard Grave, Armand Joulin, and Angela Fan. 2021. CCMatrix: Mining billions of high-quality parallel sentences on the web. In *Proceedings of the 59th Annual Meeting of the Association for Computational Linguistics and the 11th International Joint Conference on Natural Language Processing (Volume 1: Long Papers)*, pages 6490–6500, Online. Association for Computational Linguistics.

Rico Sennrich, Barry Haddow, and Alexandra Birch. 2016. Improving neural machine translation models with monolingual data. In *Proceedings of the 54th Annual Meeting of the Association for Computational Linguistics (Volume 1: Long Papers)*, pages 86–96, Berlin, Germany. Association for Computational Linguistics.

Jiatong Shi, Jonathan D. Amith, Rey Castillo García, Esteban Guadalupe Sierra, Kevin Duh, and Shinji Watanabe. 2021. Leveraging end-to-end ASR for endangered language documentation: An empirical study on yolóxochitl Mixtec. In *Proceedings of the 16th Conference of the European Chapter of the Association for Computational Linguistics: Main Volume*, pages 1134–1145, Online. Association for Computational Linguistics.

Kristine Stenzel. 2005. Multilingualism: Northwest Amazonia Revisited. In *Proceedings of the Second Annual Congress CILLA (Congreso de Idiomas Indígenas de Latinoamérica)*.

Kristine Stenzel. 2013. *A Reference Grammar of Kotiria (Wanano)*. University of Nebraska Press.

Kristine Stenzel. 2014. The pleasures and pitfalls of a 'participatory' documentation project: an experience in northwestern Amazonia. *Language documentation & conservation*, 8:287–306.

Kristine Stenzel and Nicholas Williams. 2021. Toward an interactional approach to multilingualism: Ideologies and practices in the northwest Amazon. *Language & communication*, 80:136–164.

Ilya Sutskever, Oriol Vinyals, and Quoc V Le. 2014. Sequence to sequence learning with neural networks. *Advances in neural information processing systems*, 27.

Yuqing Tang, Chau Tran, Xian Li, Peng-Jen Chen, Naman Goyal, Vishrav Chaudhary, Jiatao Gu, and Angela Fan. 2021. Multilingual translation from denoising pre-training. In *Findings of the Association for Computational Linguistics: ACL-IJCNLP 2021*, pages 3450–3466, Online. Association for Computational Linguistics.

Antonio Toral, Martijn Wieling, and Andy Way. 2018. Post-editing effort of a novel with statistical and neural machine translation. *Frontiers in Digital Humanities*, page 9.

Ashish Vaswani, Noam Shazeer, Niki Parmar, Jakob Uszkoreit, Llion Jones, Aidan N Gomez, Łukasz Kaiser, and Illia Polosukhin. 2017. Attention is all you need. *Advances in neural information processing systems*, 30.

Zhen Yang, Wei Chen, Feng Wang, and Bo Xu. 2018. Unsupervised domain adaptation for neural machine translation. In *2018 24th International Conference on Pattern Recognition (ICPR)*, pages 338–343. IEEE.

Automatic Detection of Borrowings in Low-Resource Languages of the Caucasus: Andic branch

Konstantin Zaitsev **Anzhelika Minchenko**

HSE University

knzaytsev@edu.hse.ru aminchenko@edu.hse.ru

Abstract

Linguistic borrowings occur in all languages. Andic languages of the Caucasus have borrowings from different donor-languages like Russian, Arabic, Persian. To automatically detect these borrowings, we propose a logistic regression model. The model was trained on the dataset which contains words in IPA from dictionaries of Andic languages. To improve model's quality, we compared TfIdf and Count vectorizers and chose the second one. Besides, we added new features to the model. They were extracted using analysis of vectorizer features and using a language model. The model was evaluated by classification quality metrics (precision, recall and F1-score). The best average F1-score of all languages for words in IPA was about 0.78. Experiments showed that our model reaches good results not only with words in IPA but also with words in Cyrillic.

1 Introduction

Field linguistics develops and practises methods for obtaining information about a language unknown (or little known) to the researcher based on work with native speakers. Such languages are called low-resource languages; they represent a group of languages for which the development of information technology is insufficient. There are a number of criteria (for example, speech processing, speech recognition, automatic translation, and others) according to which experts classify specific languages as low-resource.

Lexical borrowings are very common to languages, including those with few resources; this phenomenon is caused by interlingual interaction and influence. If borrowings from languages with limited resources (for example, Botlikh) are effectively identified, then automatic detection of borrowings with a universal base for related languages can be created and used. This article studies the method of identifying borrowings in low-resource Andic languages on a linguistic basis. It implies that the model imitates the borrowing rules in the receiving language based on identifying the most relevant n-grams and generating words based on the identified borrowing patterns.

Many tools for working with Andic languages are currently being developed, such as morphological parsers. Even though each language is unique and has linguistic properties, all of them are underprivileged and endangered, as the number of their speakers is constantly decreasing, and transmission from generation to generation becomes unstable. That makes developing any NLP tools essential as it can help in their further exploration and potential revival. In addition, the detection of borrowings will help to study the language more deeply and try to preserve its identity. In the future, the work could be used to create a universal transliteration so that as many linguists as possible could work with languages and, for example, with texts.

The paper's main goal is to explore the possibility of automatic borrowing detection without the usage of a bilingual dictionary since automation can contribute to future field studies of target languages. The limited amount of available data complicates the situation by reducing the number of possible analysis methods that can be implemented. The first task was to analyze the existing dictionaries. The analysis showed that the dictionaries had duplicates, which were later removed. After removing duplicates, the general borrowing rules were determined and a baseline was written with further verification of its quality. The next step was to calculate and describe insights that helped to improve the quality of the baseline. As a result, previous steps helped to cope with implementing a language model for generating additional features. To assess the quality, it was

Proceedings of the first workshop on NLP applications to field linguistics, pages 34–41
July 5–10, 2020. ©2020 Association for Computational Linguistics
https://doi.org/10.26615/978-954-452-056-4_004

necessary to perform tasks such as writing a quality metric for the language model and statistical analysis of features. These steps will be discussed in more detail in the following sections.

The rest of the article is structured as follows: the second section briefly overviews the target languages and their problems. After that, the review of the relevant literature in computational linguistics continues. The third section describes the methodology and strategies that have been used to implement the structures of each language. The fourth and fifth sections evaluate and discuss the results obtained from the available language data. The conclusion also discusses the problems that have occurred in working on the model, as well as a short description of plans for the future.

2 Literature review

2.1 Low resource language

The term "low-resource languages" (or under-resourced languages) was initially proposed by the Dutch scientist S. Krauwer. This concept refers to natural languages with some (or all) of the following properties (Vincent, B., 2004):

- the lack of their writing system or stable spelling;
- lack of qualified linguists and translators for the given language;
- limited distribution on the Internet;
- lack of electronic resources for language and speech processing, including monolingual corpora, bilingual electronic dictionaries, spelling and phonetic transcriptions of speech, pronunciation dictionaries, and more.

2.2 Theories of borrowing analysis

The term "borrowing" refers to complete language change, a diachronic process that once began as an individual innovation but then spread throughout the speech community. The most common borrowing theories for under-resourced languages are based on language rules or systems based on the constraints of those rules. While a constraint-based system basically ends up within optimality theory, rules describe how adaptation occurs and is set according to a particular borrowed word in the language's phonology (Jacobs, H., & Gussenhoven, C., 2000). Therefore, rules must be added for each specific borrowing, considering the functional aspect of speech. In addition, the rule-based model only includes rules for a particular language, so each language needs either a separate word adaptation system or a family-wide one.

A constraint-based system is analogous to a rule-based system. Constraints are included in the Optimality Theory (OT) structure. Basically, all studies of borrowings are based on this system (Turchin, P., 2010). In a constraint-based system, several constraints are defined and ranked. The input of the model is the source word with its pronunciation in the source language.

As for research in the field of borrowings by computer linguists, there are several main approaches. They can be based on both neural networks and the Optimality Theory. Neural networks are used to determine loanwords in the Uyghur language (low resource) in (Mi et al., 2018). The authors used a recurrent neural network with BiLSTM architecture, training it on a dataset with borrowings in the Uighur language. As a result, the model showed promising results, as presented in Table 1 (Mi et al., 2018). "Chn", "rus" and "arab" suffixes mean Chinese, Russian and Arabic languages respectively.

For lexical borrowings, OT is also used. The usage of OT is described in (Tsvetkov, Y., & Dyer, C., 2016). Authors' implemented model was based on OT, and it used various restrictions for Swahili, which contains borrowings from Arabic (Table 2). Similar restrictions the model uses allow one to get better results compared to simple implementations of borrowing detection.

As for neural network approaches, a possible problem is a lack of sufficient data and the need for

Model	Pchn	Rchn	F1chn	Prus	Rrus	F1rus	Parab	Rarab	F1arab
CRFs	69.78	62.33	66.35	71.64	63.25	67.18	72.50	65.32	68.72
SSIM	66.32	77.28	71.38	75.39	70.02	72.61	73.76	67.51	70.50
CIBM	78.82	68.30	73.18	81.03	73.22	76.93	75.22	70.71	72.90
RNN	78.97	79.20	79.08	82.55	75.93	79.10	83.26	77.58	80.32
Ours	**80.24**	**81.02**	**80.63**	**82.95**	**76.30**	**79.49**	**84.09**	**78.28**	**81.08**

Table 1. Experimental results of borrowings identification models based on a recurrent neural network with BiLSTM architecture.

/ ɛg/	DEP-IO	MAX-IO	ONSET	NO-CODA
a. ☞ ɛg			*	*
b. ɛgə	*!		*	
c. ɛ		*!	*	
d. ʔɛg	*!			*

Table 2. Restrictions for Swahili in the study by Tsvetkov and Dyer.

enormous computing power. In addition, OT has the disadvantage of building restriction systems for each Andic language. Such an approach will not have universality property, and its implementation will take a long time. For these reasons, we have chosen a baseline based on logistic regression, which will be presented later in the paper.

2.3 Materials for research

The collection of Andic language dictionaries (Moroz, G. et al., 2021) is used as a dataset. In total, at the moment, it contains nine (9) languages; however, for our study, we analyze only eight (8) of them since there is not enough data for the Tokita for a full-fledged study. The dataset contains two Botlikh dictionaries used in the work as sources for one language, without separation. Table 3 shows the glottocode of the language (a bibliographic database of obscure languages), its name, and the number of words in it.

Glottocode	Language	Number of Words
akhv1239	Akhvakh	14007
andi1255	Andi	6144
bagv1239	Bagvalal	12706
botl1242	Botlikh	21483
cham1309	Chamalal	9721
ghod1238	Godoberi	7423
kara1474	Karata	6650
tind1238	Tindi	12419

Table 3. Glottocode of low-resource Andic languages.

Each word in the database contains a form translated into the International Phonetic Alphabet (IPA), its canonical form (lemma), and an indication of whether the word is borrowed or not (bor). In turn, each borrowing has a short description, indicating the language from which the word came (borrowing_source_language). Some words can have different meanings or borrowing source languages. To make the task easier, we dropped duplicates and kept last occurrence of the dropped word. This approach is not quite accurate, but the number of such cases is very low. Column "meaning_ru" is written in Russian but for this paper it has an English translation. All data was collected by authors of the dataset, so we did not make any transliteration, normalization and so on. An example of a dataset with important columns for the model is presented in Table 4.

3 Method

3.1 Baseline training

The dataset presented in the previous section is at the heart of our research into language patterns and baseline learning. Since the task is to determine borrowing, models for classification are suitable for this. Also, words in IPA will be used to train the model, as they give a cleaner characteristic of borrowing. In addition, most of the work is done in the IPA, as it, unlike transcription in Cyrillic, marks the sounds of the language, which helps to conduct a cleaner analysis.

Of all classifier models, logistic regression was chosen. We decided to use TfIdf Vectorizer to transform list of words in IPA to matrix with tf-idf weights. In this matrix rows are input words and columns are symbol n-grams of each input word. To work correctly with these words, we wrote the specific token pattern that removes hyphens and splits word to IPA-symbols. In addition, we added from 2 to 4 n-grams to n-grams hyperparameter of the vectorizer. The resulting combination of models was trained in each dataset language. Training took place on the training set, validation on the test set,

lemma	ipa	glottocode	bor	borrowing_source_language	meaning_ru
аба'далIи	a-b-'a-d-a-t-ɬː-i	akhv1239	1	arab	Eternal
а/б/а'жве	a-b-'a-ʒʷ-e	akhv1239	0	NaN	everlasting
а/б/ажу'рулъIа	a-b-a-ʒ-'u-r-u-t-ɬ-a	akhv1239	0	NaN	communicate

Table 4. Dictionary description for the Akhvakh language.

Language	Precision	Recall	F1
Ahvakh	0.90	0.57	0.60
Andi	0.80	0.56	0.58
Bagvalal	0.81	0.60	0.63
Botlikh	0.88	0.74	0.78
Chamalal	0.97	0.51	0.50
Godoberi	0.89	0.61	0.65
Karata	0.96	0.51	0.49
Tindi	0.97	0.53	0.54

Table 5. Metrics for Andic languages obtained after training the baseline.

while the partition was based on the 80/20 principle. The macro average f1-score metric was used to assess the model's quality since the classes in the dataset are not balanced. After training and testing the models, it turned out that their quality was low. It was easier for Baseline to say that a word was not borrowing than the other way around. The metrics for this model for each language can be seen in Table 5.

3.2 Selection of hyperparameters

Since the baseline quality turned out to be poor, the next step was to select hyperparameters using heuristics for the vectorization model. We decided to use CountVectorizer instead of TfIdfVectorizer. This decision was based on several experiments with the same hyperparameters. CountVectorizer works like TfIdfVectorizer except for output. The output of CountVectorizer is the matrix of counted words. We added hyperparameters (min_df = 0.001, max_df = 0.1) responsible for filtering rare and frequent n-grams to get rid of noise. The number of features limitation was also removed. Experiments showed that chosen hyperparameter values are the most optimal for the model.

This implementation of the vectorization model significantly increased the model's quality, but in some languages, the F1-score remained low. To fix this problem, we analyzed the n-grams (or features) from the vectorizer matrix. The analysis showed that some of the features contribute the most to the model's quality. From these features we selected some of them which value corresponds to the set hyperparameters. Then we filtered part of selected features by a threshold value. It allowed us to select features more like the borrowing patterns we studied in languages. For each word in the dataset, it was determined whether n-grams are included in this list of features. We added a positive coefficient for the word in the case of such a feature in the n-gram of the word. The optimal coefficients and hyperparameters were selected by experiments. As a result, this approach allowed us to improve the model by small values. In the next sections this model is called as BF (baseline with features). Table 6 presents the quality metrics for the model.

3.3 Language model approach

Borrowings are characterized by the fact that they may contain those phonemes that are not typical for the receiving language, which belongs to OOV (out of vocabulary). Accordingly, such sequences may indicate that the word is borrowed. This knowledge underlies the model built on the language model on Markov chains (on n-grams), which was implemented at the next stage of the study. For the language model, a perplexity metric (Jurafsky, D., & Martin, J., 2009) was also developed to evaluate the similarities of a word to a language.

Since perplexity shows how unfamiliar the word is for the model, it can be said that the model

Language	Precision	Recall	F1
Ahvakh	0.79	0.72	0.74
Andi	0.75	0.69	0.71
Bagvalal	0.80	0.71	0.74
Botlikh	0.86	0.83	0.85
Chamalal	0.80	0.65	0.70
Godoberi	0.82	0.77	0.79
Karata	0.76	0.65	0.69
Tindi	0.73	0.65	0.68

Table 6. Metrics for Andic languages obtained after selecting hyperparameters.

trained on the language will have a lower perplexity value for non-borrowings than for borrowings. For verification, an auxiliary dataset was collected, consisting of the perplexities of each word. The language model was trained for each language of the initial dataset. The model calculated the perplexity value for the input word over several n-grams. After the calculation, the value was written to the dataset, which consisted of a word in the IPA, a lemma, a borrowing label, and perplexity values for each n-gram.

When splitting the dataset by language, we got results that visually confirmed the hypothesis. Moreover, the Wilcoxon-Mann-Whitney nonparametric statistical test confirmed the hypothesis about high perplexity of borrowing words put forward; at the same time, it can be seen that the differences in perplexities are most pronounced for trigrams. Visualization is shown in Figure 1.

The difference between perplexities further helped to implement a model that, according to trigrams, speaks of borrowing. In our study, we conducted experiments that showed that trigrams work better than bigrams (four-grams were not considered due to the identical distributions). Thus, trigrams were chosen because they best represent foreign words and experiments with bigrams and trigrams. The model is based on a language model that works like those presented above. The difference is that the language model is trained on non-borrowings since borrowings are characterized by combinations of phonemes that may not be in the language.

The language model helps to get new features from words using the algorithm. Each input word is divided into trigrams, checked in the language model: if it does not have such a trigram, then the word is borrowed and is set some positive coefficient that was selected by experiments. Otherwise, the highlighted word has a negative rate. With the help of that algorithm, a list of borrowing marks was collected for each word and added to other features.

3.4 Combining Models

Implicit knowledge of phoneme sequences can improve a regression model, as it can sometimes generate false positives on its own. For example, suppose some algorithm generates a word produced by a language model trained on borrowings. In that case, it may be borrowing since it contains a sequence of phonemes that are not in the language, although the opposite was meant. Alternatively, there may be such a situation when the language model does not have many examples. In this case, the probability of error also increases. For these reasons, additional knowledge about the language (in this case, the use of regression) can improve the results.

To implement such a model, we combined the results of the regression and trained language model. As a result, the model began to work better, although, in some languages, the quality decreased

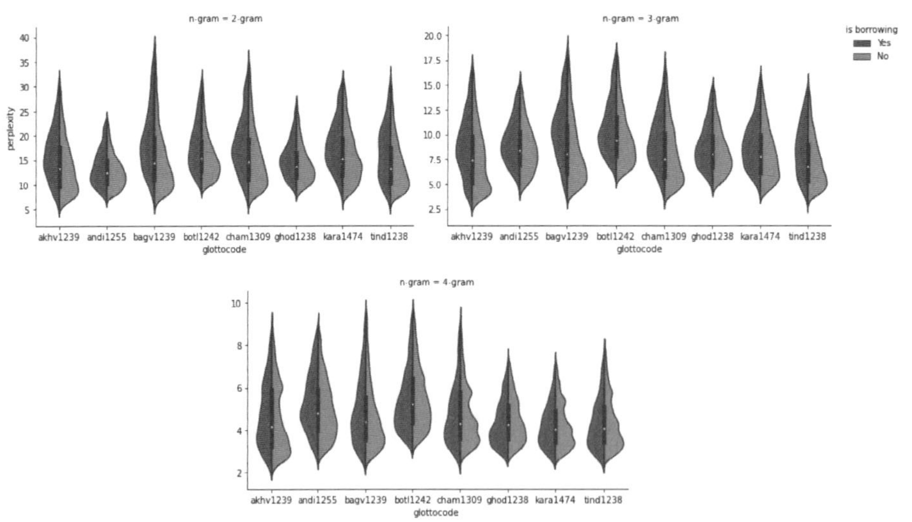

Figure 1. Graphs of the obtained results of perplexity.

Language	Precision	Recall	F1
Ahvakh	0.75	0.83	0.78
Andi	0.72	0.76	0.74
Bagvalal	0.78	0.82	0.80
Botlikh	0.80	0.88	0.83
Chamalal	0.76	0.80	0.78
Godoberi	0.78	0.86	0.81
Karata	0.70	0.73	0.71
Tindi	0.70	0.77	0.73

Table 7. Cross-validation results.

slightly compared to the previous model. The model was tested on test split, but the hyperparameters were fitted by K-fold validation, which showed high quality. The cross-validation results can be seen in Table 7.

4 Results

In addition to learning words in the IPA, the model was also trained on lemmas (BFLMlem). This experiment was carried out to compare the purity of words written in phonemes and graphemes. As a result, it turned out that the quality of the model is higher than BFLM (baseline with selected features and the language model) on IPA. Hence, the BFLM will work well for words written in IPA and Cyrillic both. A comparison of the models implemented in the article, according to the F1-score metric, is presented in Table 8.

We compared our models with others mentioned in related works. We calculate mean precision, recall, and F1-score metrics from our experiments and the results in other articles. Comparison shows that our models work slightly worse than the others, but scores remain high. Hence, simple models with feature extraction based on linguistics knowledge, such as knowing about OOV, can show results close to complicated neural network architecture models. Models' comparison is presented in Table 9.

In addition to the experiments, we tested BFLMlem on random letters and numbers. We got 0.93 mean accuracy of language models. Besides, we examined BFLM trained on IPA on English words and got 0.51 mean accuracy.

5 Discussion

In continuation of the idea of assessing perplexity in words, neural network models can be used in the future. A recurrent neural network is perfect for this. The neural network can be trained on borrowings and then generate new words and find specific patterns.

The dictionary does not fully reflect the quality of the model since it does not consider various morphological features, such as declension. For this reason, the model must be tested on work with texts. This way, it will be possible to take each word in context and determine whether it is borrowing. On the other hand, texts in languages are not presented in IPA but are written in Cyrillic. In this case, it will be possible to use the epitran tool, having previously written the rules for converting graphemes to phonemes (Mortensen, R. D., Dalmia, S., & Littell, P., 2018). In addition to the problem with the transformation, there is also the possibility that word declensions will also negatively affect the model. In general, this approach will show the actual quality of the model and can further help field linguists.

Now the model works for each language, classifying the words in it as borrowing. In the future, it may be worth refining the model, adding to it not only a binary classification but also a definition of the language from which the borrowing occurred. In this case, the problem can

Model	Akhvakh	Andi	Bagvalal	Botlikh	Chamalal	Godoberi	Karata	Tindi
Baseline	0.60	0.59	0.63	0.78	0.50	0.65	0.50	0.54
BF	0.73	0.69	0.74	0.84	0.68	0.78	0.68	0.66
BFLM	0.78	0.74	0.80	0.83	0.78	0.81	0.71	0.73
BFLMlem	**0.82**	**0.77**	**0.84**	**0.86**	**0.79**	**0.84**	**0.75**	**0.75**

Table 8. Model quality comparisons.

Model	Precision	Recall	F1
our BFLM	0.75	0.81	0.77
our BFLMlem	0.78	**0.83**	0.80
Neural Network for Uyghur	0.82	0.79	0.80
BiLSTM-CRF for Spanish	**0.91**	0.79	**0.84**

Table 9. Our models' results compare to other research.

be reformulated not within the framework of the classification but within the framework of BIO-encoding, which has already been solved for the Spanish corpus in (Alvarez-Mellado, E., & Lignos, C., 2022). Also, if we consider borrowings separately by language, it makes sense to look at the n-grams characteristic of borrowings from a particular language. Perhaps a combination of such phonemes will also speak of the source language.

In this paper, we proposed methods that can be used in a borrowings detection task. It is possible that our findings might be implemented in other models which find borrowings in low-resource languages. Besides, detected borrowings by the model might be helpful for field linguists working with Andic languages to understand deeply these languages.

6 Conclusion

This article has shown how to solve the problem of classifying borrowings in Andic low-resource languages. For this, a baseline was first used, consisting of logistic regression and TfIdf of the vectorization model. Due to unsatisfactory results, the vectorization model was changed from TfIdfVectorizer to CountVectorizer, and hyperparameters were selected for it. In addition, a simple model based on implicit language knowledge was written. After combining these models, the quality has improved significantly. As a result, our models have scores close to neural network solutions. Hence, simple binary classification can be used in tasks such as detecting borrowings. However, since the model solves a binary classification problem, it cannot tell the origin of the borrowing. In the future, it is planned to supplement the model by teaching it to solve either the problem of multiclass classification or BIO-encoding. For these problems, the future models can be based on the already implemented. Code and research are available on the GitHub repository[1].

[1] `https://github.com/Knzaytsev/Borrow-Detection`

References

Alvarez-Mellado, E., & Lignos, C., 2022. Detecting Unassimilated Borrowings in Spanish: An Annotated Corpus and Approaches to Modeling. *Proceedings of the 60th Annual Meeting of the Association for Computational Linguistics, 1*, 3868–3888.

Haspelmath, M., 2008. Loanword typology: Steps toward a systematic crosslinguistic study of lexical borrowability.

Jacobs, H., & Gussenhoven, C., 2000. Understanding phonology. *Language, 76*(1), 209. https://doi.org/10.2307/417430

List, J., Moran, S., & Prokić, J., 2013. Automatic detection of borrowings in lexicostatistic datasets.: A workflow for automatic linguistic reconstruction. *Workshop on Quantitative Approaches to Areal Typology.*

Mi et al., 2018. A Neural Network Based Model for Loanword Identification in Uyghur. *Proceedings of the Eleventh International Conference on Language Resources and Evaluation (LREC 2018).*

Moroz, G. et al., 2021. Comparative Andic dictionary database, v. 0.5 Moscow: Linguistic Convergence Laboratory, HSE University. Available from: https://github.com/phon-dicts-project/comparative_andic_dictionary_database. DOI: 10.5281/zenodo.4782876

Jurafsky, D., & Martin, J., 2009. *Speech and Language Processing (2nd Edition)*. Prentice-Hall, Inc., USA.

Mortensen, R. D., Dalmia, S., & Littell, P., 2018. Epitran: Precision G2P for Many Languages. Proceedings of the Eleventh International Conference on Language Resources and Evaluation (LREC 2018).

Tsvetkov, Y., & Dyer, C., 2016. Cross-lingual bridges with models of lexical borrowing. *Journal of Artificial Intelligence Research, 55*, 63–93. https://doi.org/10.1613/jair.4786

Turchin, P., 2010. Analyzing genetic connections between languages by matching consonant classes.

Vincent, B., 2004. Methods to computerize "little equipped" languages and groups of languages.

The interaction between cognitive ease and informativeness shapes the lexicons of natural languages

Thomas Brochhagen* **Gemma Boleda*** †

*Universitat Pompeu Fabra
†ICREA
{firstname.surname}@upf.edu

1 Introduction

Across languages, it is common for words to be associated with multiple meanings. Moreover, certain meanings are expressed by the same form more often than others (Jackson et al., 2019; Xu et al., 2020). For instance, the colexification –i.e., the conventional association of multiple meanings with the same form– of TOE and FINGER is found in at least 135 languages (Rzymski et al., 2020). These languages are spoken throughout the world and span multiple unrelated language families.

Recent research suggests that semantic relatedness increases colexification likelihood (Xu et al., 2020). Semantic memory may favor colexifying meanings that are easy to relate to one another. This, in turn, may aid vocabulary acquisition, lexical retrieval and interpretation. Building on these findings, we investigate the interplay between this and another major force: pressure for the lexicon to be informative, in the sense of supporting accurate information transfer (e.g., Regier et al., 2015). We hypothesize that languages strike a balance between these two forces. In particular, we expect colexification likelihood to increase with semantic relatedness, until a point is reached at which meanings are too related; for these highly related meanings, we expect pressure for informativeness to counteract the increasing trend, because these meanings would not be easy to disambiguate even in context. We find support for this hypothesis in two large scale analyses.[1]

2 Analysis 1

To study the relationship between semantic relatedness and colexification, we fit three generalized additive logistic models to colexification data spanning over 1200 languages and more than 1400 meanings, totaling 203056 data points. This data comes from CLICS^3 (Rzymski et al., 2020), the largest cross-linguistic database of colexifications available to date. The models characterize how likely a pair of meanings is to colexify in a given language as a function of one of three data-induced estimates of relatedness: distributional similarity, using pre-trained embeddings (Grave et al., 2018); associativity data (De Deyne et al., 2018); and the first principal component of these two measures (PC1). Both distributional and associative information are based on Dutch and English glosses of the meanings found in CLICS^3; that is, Dutch and English words are used as surrogates for meanings to estimate the latter's relatedness. Since language contact and common linguistic ancestry influence colexification (Jackson et al., 2019; Xu et al., 2020), the models are also passed information about how often a pair of meanings colexifies in other languages. This information is weighted by the phylogenetic/geographic distance to the response language. An indicator codifies whether a relatedness estimate stems from Dutch or English data.

Model comparison using approximate leave-one-out cross-validation suggests that PC1 is the best predictor of colexification, with a difference of -715 in expected log pointwise predictive density to the second highest ranked model. Figure 1 shows its estimated marginal effects. These results largely support to our hypothesis: colexification increases with relatedness until meanings are "too related", which makes their colexification decrease. Note, however, that the data are also consistent with a plateau rather than a decrease for highly related meanings (see shaded area in the figure). This is still consistent with the main hypothesis – informativeness counteracting simplicity for highly related meanings–, with a smaller effect of informativeness than we had expected.

[1]This abstract is based on the following article: Brochhagen, T., G. Boleda. 2022. When do languages use the same word for different meanings? The Goldilocks Principle in colexification. *Cognition*, Volume 226, 105179. Available at https://doi.org/10.1016/j.cognition.2022.105179.

Proceedings of the first workshop on NLP applications to field linguistics, pages 42–44
July 5–10, 2020. ©2020 Association for Computational Linguistics
https://doi.org/10.26615/978-954-452-056-4_005

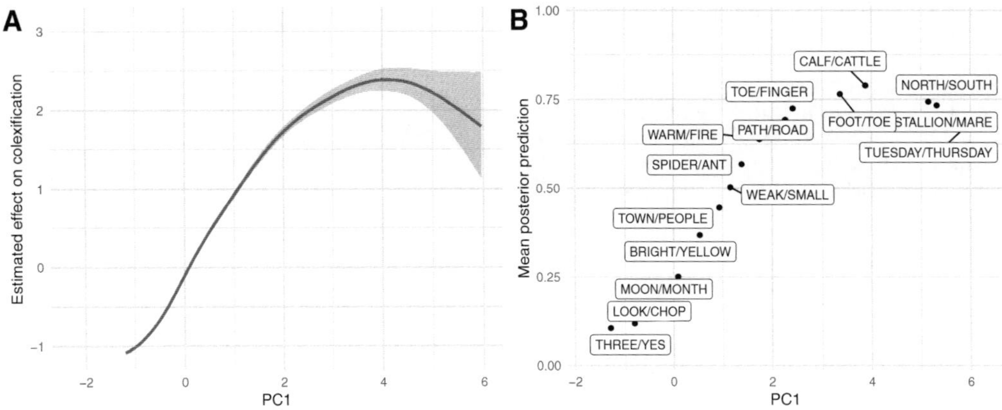

Figure 1: A: Marginal effects of standardized PC1. Shading shows 95% credible intervals. The smooth function $s(\cdot)$ characterizes how PC1's contribution to colexification likelihood changes across values. B: Mean posterior predictions for exemplary meaning pairs across PC1 values.

3 Analysis 2

Our hypothesis specifically predicts that the decrease in colexification likelihood for highly related meanings is due to their confusability. We next probe confusability more directly, focusing on the kind of relationship meanings stand in.

Pressure for informativeness should make colexifying opposites (e.g., LEFT and RIGHT) less likely than colexifying meanings in other kinds of relationships. Opposite meanings express contrasts, being maximally similar in every respect but one (e.g., Kliegr and Zamazal, 2018). Therefore, losing the distinction they encode can be expected to be particularly harmful in communicative terms. We compare opposites to meaning pairs standing in two semantic relations that do not necessarily lead to high confusability: part-whole (e.g., TOE-FOOT) and subsumption (e.g., CALF-CATTLE).

Colexification rates were estimated from 1416 meanings and 2279 languages from CLICS^3. Semantic relations are from WordNet (Fellbaum, 2015), using English words as proxies for meanings. Pairs in none of the three relations were classified as 'none/other'. As expected, this group has the lowest mean percentage of colexification (0.06, with a 95% CI of $[0.06, 0.06]$), followed by opposites (1.4 $[1.3, 1.5]$), then by subsumption (3.1 $[3.0, 3.3]$) and part-whole pairs (3.7 $[3.5, 3.8]$). These results suggest, first, that standing in one of the three relations increases the odds for meanings to colexify compared to 'none/other'; and second, that not all relations are equally conducive to colexification, with opposites being less likely to colexify.

We thus again find that relatedness makes colexification more likely, but that the need to distinguish confusable meanings can counteract this trend. Under our interpretation, simplicity makes colexification likelihood for opposites increase, whereas informativeness makes them decrease, resulting in their position in the middle compared to the other relations.

4 Conclusions

A growing body of research supports the idea that languages are efficient in the sense that they strike a good balance between informativeness and simplicity (e.g., Christiansen and Chater, 2008; Regier et al., 2015). Our large scale analyses suggest such a balance in the lexicon. We find that colexification likelihood increases with semantic relatedness, until an inflection point is reached, after which it decreases or flattens out (Analysis 1). This shift may be a consequence of a need for meanings to be distinguishable in context (Analysis 2).

References

Morten H. Christiansen and Nick Chater. 2008. Language as shaped by the brain. *BBS*, 31(05).

Simon De Deyne, Danielle J. Navarro, Amy Perfors, Marc Brysbaert, and Gert Storms. 2018. The "Small World of Words" English word association norms for over 12,000 cue words. *BRM*, 51(3):987–1006.

Christiane Fellbaum. 2015. *WordNet*. OUP.

Edouard Grave, Piotr Bojanowski, Prakhar Gupta, Armand Joulin, and Tomas Mikolov. 2018. Learning word vectors for 157 languages. In *Proc. LREC*.

Joshua C. Jackson, Joseph Watts, Teague R. Henry, Johann-Mattis List, Robert Forkel, Peter J. Mucha, Simon J. Greenhill, Russell D. Gray, and Kristen A. Lindquist. 2019. Emotion semantics show both cultural variation and universal structure. *Science*.

Tomáš Kliegr and Ondřej Zamazal. 2018. Antonyms are similar: Towards paradigmatic association approach to rating similarity in SimLex-999 and WordSim-353. *DKE*, 115:174–193.

Terry Regier, Charles Kemp, and Paul Kay. 2015. *Word Meanings across Languages Support Efficient Communication*, chapter 11. John Wiley & Sons, Ltd.

Christoph Rzymski, Tiago Tresoldi, Simon J Greenhill, Mei-Shin Wu, et al. 2020. The database of cross-linguistic colexifications, reproducible analysis of cross-linguistic polysemies. *Sci. Data*, 7(1):1–12.

Yang Xu, Khang Duong, Barbara C Malt, Serena Jiang, and Mahesh Srinivasan. 2020. Conceptual relations predict colexification across languages. *Cognition*.

The first neural machine translation system for the Erzya language

David Dale*
dale.david@yandex.ru

Abstract

We present the first neural machine translation system for translation between the endangered Erzya language and Russian and the dataset collected by us to train and evaluate it. The BLEU scores are 17 and 19 for translation to Erzya and Russian respectively, and more than half of the translations are rated as acceptable by native speakers. We also adapt our model to translate between Erzya and 10 other languages, but without additional parallel data, the quality on these directions remains low. We release the translation models along with the collected text corpus, a new language identification model, and a multilingual sentence encoder adapted for the Erzya language.

1 Introduction

Out of the 7 thousand languages spoken around the world, only a minor fraction is covered by machine translation tools. For example, Google Translate[1] supports only 133 languages, and a recent model by NLLB Team et al. (2022) supports 202 languages. Most other languages are often considered "low-resource", although some of them have millions of native speakers. In the context of machine translation, the resources that are low are, primarily, parallel and monolingual text corpora. In this work, we create a machine translation system for the previously uncovered Erzya language with only publicly available resources, a very small budget, and limited human efforts. We hope that it will inspire researchers and language activists to enlarge the coverage of existing NLP resources, and in particular, translation systems.

Our language of choice is Erzya (myv), which is spoken primarily in the Republic of Mordovia, located in the center of the European part of the Russian Federation. The language, along with its close relative Moksha (mdf), belongs to the Mordvinic branch of the Uralic language family. These two languages, although not mutually intelligible (Janurik, 2017), are often referred to under the common name "Mordovian". Erzya has had a written tradition since the beginning of the 19th century (Rueter, 2013). Its most widely used alphabet is Cyrillic, although there is a Latin-based alternative alphabet[2]. Erzya has supposedly 300 thousand speakers[3], and it is one of the three official languages in Mordovia. According to the UNESCO classification, the Erzya language has a status of "definitely endangered" (UNESCO, 2010). Some researchers (Janurik, 2017) put it between the levels 6b ("threatened") and 7 ("shifting") on the EGIDS scale (Lewis and Simons, 2010), as it is widely used and transmitted between generations in rural communities but is being gradually displaced by Russian in urban areas. More details about the use of Erzya are given by Rueter (2013), who is also a major current contributor to Erzya NLP resources.

As far as we know, prior to this work, no neural machine translation (NMT) systems for Erzya have been published. To fill this gap, we create and publicly release[4] the following deliverables:

- A language identification model with enhanced recall for Erzya and Moksha languages;
- A sentence encoder for Erzya compatible with LaBSE (Feng et al., 2022);
- A small parallel Erzya-Russian corpus and a larger monolingual Erzya corpus;
- Two neural models for translation between Erzya and 11 other languages.

For translation between Russian and Erzya, we validate our models both by automatic metrics and with judgments of native speakers. More than half

*The research was conducted between the author's employments at Skolkovo Institute of Science and Technology (Skoltech) and at Meta AI.

[1]https://translate.google.com

[2]http://valks.erzja.info (currently blocked in Russia)

[3]In the 2010 census, 430 thousand people reported speaking Erzya or Moksha, but their proportions are unclear.

[4]The source code and links to other resources are provided at https://github.com/slone-nlp/myv-nmt.

Proceedings of the first workshop on NLP applications to field linguistics, pages 45–53
July 5–10, 2020. ©2020 Association for Computational Linguistics
https://doi.org/10.26615/978-954-452-056-4_006

of the translations are rated as acceptable.

2 Related Work

Low-resource NLP and, in particular, machine translation, have attracted a lot of attention. Among the recent ambitious projects are Bapna et al. (2022) and NLLB Team et al. (2022) that aim at creating NMT systems for hundreds of languages and rely heavily on collection of large online corpora and transfer learning. Other works, such as Hämäläinen and Alnajjar (2019), focus on efficient use of existing vocabularies and morphosyntactic tools to train machine translation systems for very low-resourced languages.

As far as we know, there are no published large parallel corpora or NMT systems for Erzya. Rueter and Tyers (2018) develop an Erzya treebank with a few hundred translations to English and Finnish. Архангельский (2019) present an Erzya web corpus[5] along with the way it was collected, but the corpus is available only via the web interface. For other published corpora, the situation is similar. There exists a half-finished rule-based machine translation system between Erzya and Finnish[6], and a grammar parser for Erzya[7]. The software package UralicNLP (Hämäläinen, 2019) supports Erzya among other languages.

There have been a few attempts to transfer machine learning-based NLP resources to Erzya from high-resource languages. Alnajjar (2021) adapt Finnish, English, and Russian word embeddings to Erzya. Muller et al. (2021), Ács et al. (2021) and Wang et al. (2022) evaluate the performance of multilingual BERT-like models on natural language understanding tasks for new languages, including Erzya.

None of the works known to us train machine learning-based models that are capable of generating Erzya language.

3 Methodology and Experiments

3.1 Data Collection

As there are no large open-access corpora for Erzya, we compile Erzya and Erzya-Russian data from various sources:

- 12K parallel sentences from the Bible[8];
- 3K parallel Wikimedia sentences from OPUS (Tiedemann, 2012);
- 42K parallel words or short phrases collected from various online dictionaries;
- the Erzya Wikipedia and the corresponding articles from the Russian Wikipedia;
- 18 books, including 3 books with Erzya-Russian bitexts[9];
- Soviet-time books and periodicals[10];
- The Erzya part of Wikisource[11];
- Short texts by modern Erzya authors[12];
- News articles from the Erzya Pravda website[13];
- Texts found in LiveJournal[14] by searching with the 100 most frequent Erzya words.

A more detailed account of the data sources is given in Appendix A.

After filtering these texts with the language identification model (Section 3.2), we gathered 330K unique Erzya sentences. A bilingual part of the texts was used for mining additional parallel sentences in Section 3.4.

3.2 Language Identification

To make sure that the extra collected data is in the Erzya language, we train a FastText (Joulin et al., 2016) language classifier for the 323 languages present in Wikipedia. The 267 thousand training texts were sampled from Wikipedia with probabilities proportional to $n_{lang}^{1/5}$, where n_{lang} is the size of Wikipedia in that language[15]. To increase the recall for Erzya and Moksha languages, we augment this training dataset with Erzya and Moksha Bible texts. The resulting model has 89% accuracy and 86% macro F1 score on the Wikipedia test set (sampled with the same temperature). For Erzya, it has 97% precision and 82% recall. Hyperparameters for all trained models are listed in Appendix B.

3.3 Erzya Sentence Encoder

To compute sentence embeddings, we use an encoder based on LaBSE (Feng et al., 2022), with an extended vocabulary. First, we use the BPE algorithm (Sennrich et al., 2016) over a monolingual

[5]http://erzya.web-corpora.net/

[6]https://github.com/apertium/apertium-myv-fin

[7]https://github.com/timarkh/uniparser-grammar-erzya

[8]http://finugorbib.com

[9]http://lib.e-mordovia.ru

[10]https://fennougrica.kansalliskirjasto.fi

[11]https://wikisource.org/wiki/Main_Page/?oldid=895127

[12]https://rus4all.ru/myv/

[13]http://erziapr.ru

[14]https://www.livejournal.com

[15]We adopted the idea of temperature sampling with T=5 from Tran et al. (2021) and several other works.

Erzya corpus to add 19K extra merged tokens to the vocabulary. Then, we fine-tune the model on the limited initial parallel data (the Bible, OPUS, and dictionaries): we update only the token embeddings matrix, using the contrastive loss from Feng et al. (2022) over computed sentence embeddings. Finally, after collecting more parallel sentences, we fine-tune the full model on a mixture of tasks: contrastive loss over sentence embeddings, standard masked language modeling loss, and sentence pair classification to distinguish correct translations from random pairs.

3.4 Mining Parallel Sentences

When mining parallel sentences, we strive for high precision. To compensate for the questionable quality of our sentence encoder, we apply the following procedure[16].

- We perform only local mining, i.e. we compare sentences only across paired documents (for Wikipedia and translated books), or within one document (for the web sources).
- To evaluate similarity of two sentences, we multiply the cosine similarity between their LaBSE embeddings by the ratio of the length of the shortest sentence to that of the longest one.
- We further penalize the similarities by partially subtracting from them the average similarities of each sentence to its closest neighbors, similarly to using distance margin from Artetxe and Schwenk (2019).
- Given two documents in Russian and Erzya, we use dynamic programming to select a sequence of sentence pairs that have the maximal sum of pairwise similarity scores and go in the same order in both documents.
- We accept only the sentence pairs with a score above a threshold, which was manually tuned for each source of texts.

In total, this approach yielded 21K more unique parallel sentence pairs. The manual inspection found that more than 90% of them were matched correctly.

3.5 Training Machine Translation Models

To benefit from transfer learning, we base our model on the mBART50 model (Tang et al., 2020) pretrained on multiple languages, including two Uralic ones (Finnish and Estonian). We extend its BPE vocabulary with 19K new Erzya tokens, using the same method as in Section 3.3, and add a new myv_XX language code to it. Embeddings for the new tokens are initialized as the averages of the embeddings of the Russian tokens aligned with them in the parallel corpus[17], inspired by Xu and Hong (2022).

We make two copies of this model and train them to translate in the myv-ru and ru-myv directions, respectively. The myv-ru model is trained on the joint parallel corpus of sentences and words. The ru-myv model is trained on the union of this corpus and the back-translated corpus generated by the myv-ru model from the monolingual myv data.

After training the models on these two languages, we adapt them to 10 more languages: ar, de, en, es, fi, fr, hi, tr, uk, and zh, resulting in the myv-mul and mul-myv models (below, by mul we denote any of these 10 languages). We fine-tune the two models jointly, using a version of online-back translation and self-training. Specifically, we generate the training pairs in four alternating steps:

1. Sample a ru-mul sentence pair from the CCMatrix (Schwenk et al., 2021) dataset, translate from ru to myv with the mul-myv model;
2. Sample a ru-mul pair from the CCMatrix, translate from mul to myv with the mul-myv model;
3. Sample a ru-myv pair from our parallel corpus, translate from myv to mul with the myv-mul model;
4. Sample a myv text from the monolingual myv corpus, translate from mul to myv and ru with the myv-mul model.

At each step, we update both models on the myv-mul and myv-ru pairs in both directions. For the self-training updates, we multiply the loss by the coefficient $\lambda_{ST} = 0.05$ to decrease the impact of self-training relatively to back-translation (the choice of the coefficient is suggested by experiments in He et al. (2022)).

During the initial experiments, we noticed that, when translating from Russian to Erzya, the model often just copied Russian phrases with only word

[16]For more details on the mining procedure, please read the source code in the repository that we release.

[17]We compute alignments with a naive formula: the alignment weight between tokens t_i and t_j is estimated as $\frac{n_{ij}^2}{n_j n_j}$, where n_i and n_j are their respective frequencies in the parallel corpus, and n_{ij} is the number of sentence pairs with t_i in one sentence and t_j in another.

endings sometimes changed. Sometimes this is acceptable because Erzya has multiple Russian loanwords, but often there exist native words that are preferable. To alleviate this problem, in step 1 we generate 5 alternative ru-myv translations using diverse beam search (Vijayakumar et al., 2016), and choose the one with the largest proportion of words recognized as myv by our language identification model. This problem was also the reason why we chose to train two different models from translation to Erzya and from Erzya: this way, the decoder and encoder of a model never work with the same language.

Direction	BLEU	ChrF++
ru-myv	17.71	41.16
myv-ru	19.68	38.63
en-myv	2.77	28.03
myv-en	5.44	25.99
fi-myv	4.79	27.42
myv-fi	3.02	22.34

Table 1: Reference-based scores on the test sets.

	ru-myv		myv-ru	
Source	**BLEU**	**ChrF++**	**BLEU**	**ChrF++**
bible	10.00	36.92	10.71	33.55
tales	7.00	33.90	7.30	28.42
constitution	27.82	62.96	33.31	60.60
games	10.33	31.19	9.85	26.57
fiction	8.68	30.59	5.95	26.60
wiki	28.39	48.56	32.24	47.55

Table 2: Scores by section on the myv-ru test set.

4 Evaluation

4.1 Data

For model evaluation, we prepare a held-out corpus of 3000 aligned Erzya-Russian sentences from 6 diverse sources: the Bible, Erzya folk tales (Sheyanova, 2017), the Soviet 1938 constitution, descriptions of folk children's games (Брыжинский, 2009), modern Erzya fiction and poetry, and Wikipedia. To evaluate English and Finnish translation, we use translations from the Erzya universal-dependency treebank (Rueter and Tyers, 2018): 441 sentence pairs for en, and 309 for fi. We split all these sets into development and test parts, and report the results on the test set.

4.2 Automatic Metrics

For all evaluated directions (between myv and ru, en, fi) we calculate BLEU (Papineni et al., 2002) and ChrF++ (Popović, 2017). Both these metrics estimate the proportion of common parts in the translation and the reference, but BLEU is calculated as precision over word n-grams, whereas ChrF++ aggregates precision and recall of word and character n-grams (which is more suitable for morphologically rich languages such as Erzya and Russian). The values of these metrics on the test set are given in Table 1. For translation from and to Russian, the BLEU scores are 17 and 19 points, respectively. For English and Finnish, however, BLEU is well below 10. We hypothesize that the low quality may be attributed to the domain mismatch between the Erzya-origin and English- or Finnish-origin training corpora, but without detailed test sets we cannot verify this.

For the Russian test set, the performance varies greatly depending on the domain (Table 2). The constitution has the highest scores because its Erzya text is saturated with Russian loanwords and is easy to generate and understand. For Wikipedia, the scores are also high, probably because its Erzya articles are often translated from Russian in a rather literal way. The other domains have a more artistic style, and the translations are on average much less literal.

Some examples of the translations and references are given in Table 3.

4.3 Manual Evaluation

We recruit three native speaker volunteers to evaluate some translations manually. The evaluation protocol is similar to XSTS (NLLB Team et al., 2022), but evaluates fluency in addition to semantic similarity. The scores are between 1 (a useless translation) and 5 (a perfect translation), with 3 points standing for an acceptable translation without serious errors. Criteria for each score are given in Appendix C.

Each of the 3 annotators rated a few randomly sampled translations from the dev split of each source: 12 pairs in the ru-myv and 17 pairs in the myv-ru directions, which amounts to 87 sentence pairs annotations in total. The average length of the labelled texts was 97 characters, or 14 words.

It turned out that, despite the specified annotation criteria, the annotators were calibrated very differently: their average ratings were 2.9, 3.5, and 4.1. We chose a pessimistic aggregation strategy: for each of the 29 evaluated sentence pairs, we took the worst of the scores by our 3 volunteers.

For translation to Erzya, the average pessimistic score was 2.75, and 58% translations were rated as acceptable (i.e. all the 3 reviewers rated them

Type	Text
source (ru)	И вот что рассказывают наши русские старики: «Когда здесь не было этого села, в этом овраге были разбойники; у них были землянки.
source (myv)	Вана мезе ёвтнить миненек рузонь атятне: зярдо велесь тесэ арасель, се латксонть эрясть розбойникть, эрясть землянкасо.
translation (ru-myv)	Ды вана мезе ёвтнить минек эрзянь атятне: «Зярдояк те велесэнть арасель, тосо оврагасо ульнесть розбойникть; сынст ульнесть землянкаст.
translation (myv-ru)	Вот что нам говорят русские старцы: когда деревня здесь не была, то там жилибойники, жили на земле.
source (myv)	Кода авазо, анокстась лапужа кирькст, истя жо педявтнинзе, валаськавтнинзе педявтома таркатнень начко кедьсэ.
source (en)	Like his mother, he prepared flat rings, and stuck them onto the patty in the same way, and smoothed out the seams with his wet hands.
source (fi)	Samalla tavalla kuin äitinsä Ketšai valmisti litteitä rinkuloita liitti ne samalla tavalla, ja siloitti liitoksen märällä kädellä.
translation (myv-en)	Like his mother, he prepared flat circles, and also filled the canvas with a needle.
translation (myv-fi)	Kuten äiti, valmistelee tasa-alaiset kentät, myös venytetään, lyödään venyttäjän käsillä.
translation (en-myv)	Кода аванзо, сон анокстыль валаня суркст, теке ладсо педявтызе сынст пацьказонзо ды вадяшась кедень летькенть марто.
translation (fi-myv)	Истя жо, кода авазо Кетшай анокстыль лангсо кевпанть, сон солодиль сынст теке ладсо ды солодиль эйсэст кедьлапушкасо.

Table 3: A few examples of translations and references.

with at least 3 points). For translation to Russian, the average score was 2.71, with 53% acceptable translations.

An additional comment from the annotators was that some of the source Erzya texts were inadequate. In particular, some games sentences contained grammatical errors[18], and most constitution sentences contained Russian words with Erzya endings instead of their Erzya equivalents. This suggests that one of the next steps in improving our NMT system might be to filter the training and evaluation data for better language quality.

5 Conclusions and Future Work

In this paper, we present the first NMT system for the endangered Erzya language, capable of translating between it and 11 diverse languages, primarily Russian. During its development, we have collected about 30K parallel Russian-Erzya sentences and 300K monolingual Erzya sentences, and trained a language identification model and a BERT-based sentence encoder that support Erzya. All the resources are publicly released. These efforts have occupied about two man-weeks of working time and almost no expenses[19]. We hope that these results will inspire the NLP community to develop resources for other endangered languages.

The quality of our system may be improved by collecting more texts in Erzya and filtering them better than we did. Another promising direction is a more efficient usage of the vocabularies and parsers that are already available for the language, e.g. for generating synthetic training data. Finally, we hope to attract more native speakers for creating larger and cleaner train and test datasets.

One open research question is that of transfer between languages: whether Erzya translation benefits from knowledge of, for example, Hungarian or Estonian, and whether knowledge of Erzya can bring improvements to other languages, such as Moksha. In further studies, we hope to shed some light on this direction as well.

6 Acknowledgements

We gratefully acknowledge support from the volunteers who participated in the manual evaluation of translation quality: Semyon Tumaikin, Zinyoronj Santyai, and Evgenia Chugunova. We are also grateful to the reviewers for their helpful suggestions which substantially improved this work.

References

Fenno-ugrica. https://fennougrica.kansalliskirjasto.fi/. Accessed: 2022-08-01.

Livejournal. https://www.livejournal.com. Accessed: 2022-08-01.

a. The wikimedia dump service. https://dumps.wikimedia.org/myvwiki/20220601/. Accessed: 2022-08-01.

[18] We are not certain whether these errors are due to the low quality of the source text, or to the natural variations within the Erzya language.

[19] All the expenses incurred totalled $9.99 for the paid subscription to the Google Colab system (https://colab.research.google.com/signup).

b. Wikisource. https://wikisource.org/wiki/Main_Page/?oldid=895127. Accessed: 2022-08-01.

Портал национальных литератур. Эрзянский язык. https://rus4all.ru/myv/. Accessed: 2022-08-01.

Эрзянь Правда. http://erziapr.ru/. Accessed: 2022-08-01.

1938. *Советской Социалистической Республикатнень Союзонь Конституциясь (Основной Законось)*. Мордгиз, Саранск.

Judit Ács, Dániel Lévai, and Andras Kornai. 2021. Evaluating transferability of BERT models on uralic languages. In *Proceedings of the Seventh International Workshop on Computational Linguistics of Uralic Languages*, pages 8–17, Syktyvkar, Russia (Online). Association for Computational Linguistics.

Khalid Alnajjar. 2021. When word embeddings become endangered. *arXiv preprint arXiv:2103.13275*.

Mikel Artetxe and Holger Schwenk. 2019. Margin-based parallel corpus mining with multilingual sentence embeddings. In *Proceedings of the 57th Annual Meeting of the Association for Computational Linguistics*, pages 3197–3203, Florence, Italy. Association for Computational Linguistics.

Ankur Bapna, Isaac Caswell, Julia Kreutzer, Orhan Firat, Daan van Esch, Aditya Siddhant, Mengmeng Niu, Pallavi Baljekar, Xavier Garcia, Wolfgang Macherey, et al. 2022. Building machine translation systems for the next thousand languages. *arXiv preprint arXiv:2205.03983*.

Fangxiaoyu Feng, Yinfei Yang, Daniel Cer, Naveen Arivazhagan, and Wei Wang. 2022. Language-agnostic BERT sentence embedding. In *Proceedings of the 60th Annual Meeting of the Association for Computational Linguistics (Volume 1: Long Papers)*, pages 878–891, Dublin, Ireland. Association for Computational Linguistics.

finugorbib.com. http://finugorbib.com/. Accessed: 2022-08-01.

Mika Hämäläinen and Khalid Alnajjar. 2019. A template based approach for training nmt for low-resource uralic languages - a pilot with finnish. In *Proceedings of the 2019 2nd International Conference on Algorithms, Computing and Artificial Intelligence*, ACAI 2019, page 520–525, New York, NY, USA. Association for Computing Machinery.

Zhiwei He, Xing Wang, Rui Wang, Shuming Shi, and Zhaopeng Tu. 2022. Bridging the data gap between training and inference for unsupervised neural machine translation. In *Proceedings of the 60th Annual Meeting of the Association for Computational Linguistics (Volume 1: Long Papers)*, pages 6611–6623, Dublin, Ireland. Association for Computational Linguistics.

Mika Hämäläinen. 2019. UralicNLP: An NLP library for Uralic languages. *Journal of Open Source Software*, 4(37):1345.

Boglárka Janurik. 2017. Erzya-russian bilingual discourse: A structural analysis of intrasentential code-switching patterns. *Szeged: Szegedi Tudományegyetem PhD dissertation. Manuscript.*

Armand Joulin, Edouard Grave, Piotr Bojanowski, and Tomas Mikolov. 2016. Bag of tricks for efficient text classification. *arXiv preprint arXiv:1607.01759*.

M Paul Lewis and Gary F Simons. 2010. Assessing endangerment: expanding fishman's gids.

lib.e mordovia.ru. http://lib.e-mordovia.ru. Accessed: 2022-08-01.

marlamuter.com. Эрзя-Руш мутер. http://marlamuter.com/muter/Эрзя. Accessed: 2022-08-01.

mordovians.ru. Русско-Эрзянский словарь. https://www.mordovians.ru/erzyanskiy_yazyk. Accessed: 2022-08-01.

mordvarf.com. Русско-Эрзянский словарь. https://mordvarf.com/русско-эрзянский-словарь/. Accessed: 2022-08-01.

Benjamin Muller, Antonios Anastasopoulos, Benoît Sagot, and Djamé Seddah. 2021. When being unseen from mBERT is just the beginning: Handling new languages with multilingual language models. In *Proceedings of the 2021 Conference of the North American Chapter of the Association for Computational Linguistics: Human Language Technologies*, pages 448–462, Online. Association for Computational Linguistics.

NLLB Team, Marta R. Costa-jussà, James Cross, Onur Çelebi, Maha Elbayad, Kenneth Heafield, Kevin Heffernan, Elahe Kalbassi, Janice Lam, Daniel Licht, Jean Maillard, Anna Sun, Skyler Wang, Guillaume Wenzek, Al Youngblood, Bapi Akula, Loic Barrault, Gabriel Mejia-Gonzalez, Prangthip Hansanti, John Hoffman, Semarley Jarrett, Kaushik Ram Sadagopan, Dirk Rowe, Shannon Spruit, Chau Tran, Pierre Andrews, Necip Fazil Ayan, Shruti Bhosale, Sergey Edunov, Angela Fan, Cynthia Gao, Vedanuj Goswami, Francisco Guzmán, Philipp Koehn, Alexandre Mourachko, Christophe Ropers, Safiyyah Saleem, Holger Schwenk, and Jeff Wang. 2022. No language left behind: Scaling human-centered machine translation.

Kishore Papineni, Salim Roukos, Todd Ward, and Wei-Jing Zhu. 2002. Bleu: a method for automatic evaluation of machine translation. In *Proceedings of the 40th Annual Meeting of the Association for Computational Linguistics*, pages 311–318, Philadelphia, Pennsylvania, USA. Association for Computational Linguistics.

Maja Popović. 2017. chrF++: words helping character n-grams. In *Proceedings of the Second Conference on Machine Translation*, pages 612–618, Copenhagen, Denmark. Association for Computational Linguistics.

Jack Rueter. 2013. The erzya language. where is it spoken? *Études finno-ougriennes*, (45).

Jack Rueter and Francis Tyers. 2018. Towards an open-source universal-dependency treebank for Erzya. In *Proceedings of the Fourth International Workshop on Computational Linguistics of Uralic Languages*, pages 106–118, Helsinki, Finland. Association for Computational Linguistics.

Holger Schwenk, Guillaume Wenzek, Sergey Edunov, Edouard Grave, Armand Joulin, and Angela Fan. 2021. CCMatrix: Mining billions of high-quality parallel sentences on the web. In *Proceedings of the 59th Annual Meeting of the Association for Computational Linguistics and the 11th International Joint Conference on Natural Language Processing (Volume 1: Long Papers)*, pages 6490–6500, Online. Association for Computational Linguistics.

Rico Sennrich, Barry Haddow, and Alexandra Birch. 2016. Neural machine translation of rare words with subword units. In *Proceedings of the 54th Annual Meeting of the Association for Computational Linguistics (Volume 1: Long Papers)*, pages 1715–1725, Berlin, Germany. Association for Computational Linguistics.

Irina Ivanovna Sheyanova. 2017. *Skaz forms of Mordovian literature*. The Research Institute of the Humanities by the Government of the Republic of Mordovia, Saransk.

Yuqing Tang, Chau Tran, Xian Li, Peng-Jen Chen, Naman Goyal, Vishrav Chaudhary, Jiatao Gu, and Angela Fan. 2020. Multilingual translation with extensible multilingual pretraining and finetuning. *arXiv preprint arXiv:2008.00401*.

Jörg Tiedemann. 2012. Parallel data, tools and interfaces in OPUS. In *Proceedings of the Eighth International Conference on Language Resources and Evaluation (LREC'12)*, pages 2214–2218, Istanbul, Turkey. European Language Resources Association (ELRA).

Chau Tran, Shruti Bhosale, James Cross, Philipp Koehn, Sergey Edunov, and Angela Fan. 2021. Facebook AI's WMT21 news translation task submission. In *Proceedings of the Sixth Conference on Machine Translation*, pages 205–215, Online. Association for Computational Linguistics.

UNESCO. 2010. Unesco atlas of the world's languages in danger (pdf).

Ashwin K Vijayakumar, Michael Cogswell, Ramprasath R Selvaraju, Qing Sun, Stefan Lee, David Crandall, and Dhruv Batra. 2016. Diverse beam search: Decoding diverse solutions from neural sequence models. *arXiv preprint arXiv:1610.02424*.

Xinyi Wang, Sebastian Ruder, and Graham Neubig. 2022. Expanding pretrained models to thousands more languages via lexicon-based adaptation. In *Proceedings of the 60th Annual Meeting of the Association for Computational Linguistics (Volume 1: Long Papers)*, pages 863–877, Dublin, Ireland. Association for Computational Linguistics.

Minhan Xu and Yu Hong. 2022. Sub-word alignment is still useful: A vest-pocket method for enhancing low-resource machine translation. In *Proceedings of the 60th Annual Meeting of the Association for Computational Linguistics (Volume 2: Short Papers)*, pages 613–619, Dublin, Ireland. Association for Computational Linguistics.

Тимофей Александрович Архангельский. 2019. Интернет-корпуса финно-угорских языков России. *Ежегодник финно-угорских исследований*, (3):528–537.

Василий Сергеевич Брыжинский. 2009. *Мордовские народные игры*. Мордовское кн. издательство, Saransk.

М.Е. Евсевьев. 1964. Мордовские народные сказки и загадки. *Евсевьев М.Е. Избранные труды.*, 3:412.

И.Н Рябов, Е.Ф. Клементьева, and Г.В. Рябова. 2011. *Эрзянский язык. Учебное пособие*. Издательство Мордовского университета, Саранск.

Валентина Ивановна Щанкина. 2011. *Русско-мокшанско-эрзянский словарь*. Поволжский центр культур финно-угорских народов, Саранск.

Борис Эрюшов. Русско-Эрзянский словарь. http://lazalyk.narod.ru/business.html. Accessed: 2022-08-01.

A Data sources

Source	Type	Size
Erzya-Russian dictionaries: marlamuter.com, mordovians.ru, mordvarf.com, Рябов et al. (2011), Щанкина (2011), Эрюшов	phrase pairs	47860
The myv-ru Wikimedia corpus on OPUS (Tiedemann, 2012)	sentence pairs	3202
The Bible (finugorbib.com)	sentence pairs	12483
Sheyanova (2017) (aligned)	sentence pairs	1023
Брыжинский (2009) (aligned)	sentence pairs	4203
Erzya and Russian Wikipedia (wik, a) (aligned)	sentence pairs	11479
Livejournal (lj) (aligned)	sentence pairs	1799
Modern Erzya fiction and poetry (rus) (aligned)	sentence pairs	916
The Soviet 1938 constitution (con, 1938) (aligned)	sentence pairs	304
Mordovian tales and riddles (Евсевьев, 1964) (aligned)	sentence pairs	3776
Various Erzya fiction books (lib.e mordovia.ru)	sentences	52870
Various Soviet-time books and periodicals (fen)	sentences	54798
Erzya Wikisource, filtered by language (wik, b)	sentences	120470
Articles from the Erzya Pravda website (pra)	sentences	43772
Livejournal (lj)	sentences	36584
Erzya Wikipedia (wik, a)	sentences	59569
Брыжинский (2009)	sentences	5194

Table 4: The sources used to construct the training and evaluation datasets. The "size" column denotes the number of sentences or phrases in the source.

B Models' hyperparameters

B.1 Language identification

For the language identification model, we use the official FastText implementation[20]. We train it with initial learning rate of 0.05 for 100 epochs, using minimum word count of 100, 64-dimensional embeddings and 200K hash buckets for character n-grams with n from 1 to 4. Then we quantize the model with retraining on the same dataset, a cutoff of 50000, and norm pruning.

B.2 Sentence encoder

For the sentence encoder model, we use a PyTorch port of LaBSE[21], in which we remove tokens for all languages, except Russian and English, and add Erzya tokens. For vocabulary extension, we set the minimal token count for stopping BPE at 30.

After extending the vocabulary, we fine-tune the model on the initial parallel sentences and phrases using the LaBSE contrastive loss with margin 0.3 and batch size 4 for 500K steps, updating only the embeddings, and passing the gradient only through the encoded myv sentence. We use the Adafactor optimizer with learning rate of 10^{-5} and clipping the gradient norm at 1. Then we update the model for 500K steps with learning rate 2×10^{-6}, updating all the parameters, and alternating batches with the LaBSE loss, MLM loss, and the loss of classifying the correct and incorrect sentence pairs. Incorrect pairs are generated either by sampling one of the sentences randomly, or by randomly inserting, deleting, or swapping words in one of the sentences in a correct parallel pair.

B.3 Machine translation models

Both myv-ru and ru-myv models were initialized from mBART50[22] with the vocabulary extended with Erzya tokens. They were trained with Adafactor optimizer using batch size of 8 and learning rate of 10^{-6}

[20] https://github.com/facebookresearch/fastText
[21] https://huggingface.co/sentence-transformers/LaBSE
[22] https://huggingface.co/facebook/mbart-large-50-many-to-many-mmt

for 4 epochs: on the first epoch, only token embeddings were updated, and on the remaining epochs, all parameters were updated.

The myv-mul and mul-myv models were initialized from myv-ru and ru-myv, respectively. They were jointly trained for 40K updates with batch size of 1.

For inference, we used beam size of 5 and repetition penalty of 5.0.

Both the sentence encoder and the translation models were trained using the PyTorch[23] and Transformers[24] Python packages.

C Quality annotation guidelines

The following annotation criteria (in Russian) were suggested to the annotators in Section 4.3.

- 5 points: a perfect translation. The meaning and the style are reproduced completely, the grammar and word choice are correct, the text looks natural.
- 4 points: a good translation. The meaning is reproduced completely or almost completely, the style and the word choice are natural for the target language.
- 3 points: an acceptable translation. The general meaning is reproduced; the mistakes in word choice and grammar do not hinder understanding; most of the text is grammatically correct and in the target language.
- 2 points: a bad translation. The text is mainly understandable and mainly in the target language, but there are critical mistakes in meaning, grammar, or word choice.
- 1 point: a useless translation. A large part of the text is in the wrong language, or is incomprehensible, or has little relation to the original text.

[23]https://pytorch.org

[24]https://huggingface.co/docs/transformers/

Abui Wordnet: Using a Toolbox Dictionary to develop a wordnet for a low-resource language

František Kratochvíl and **Luís Morgado da Costa**
Department of Asian Studies
Palacký University Olomouc
Czech Republic
frantisek.kratochvil@upol.cz and luis.morgadodacosta@upol.cz

Abstract

This paper describes a procedure to link a Toolbox dictionary of a low-resource language to correct synsets, generating a new wordnet. We introduce a bootstrapping technique utilising the information in the gloss fields (English, national, and regional) to generate sense candidates using a naive algorithm based on multilingual sense intersection. We show that this technique is quite effective when glosses are available in more than one language. Our technique complements the previous work by (Rosman et al., 2014) which linked the SIL Semantic Domains to wordnet senses. Through this work we have created a small, fully hand-checked wordnet for Abui, containing over 1,400 concepts and 3,600 senses.

1 Introduction

This paper describes the development of a wordnet for Abui, one of more than twenty Timor-Alor-Pantar languages of Eastern Indonesia. The Timor-Alor-Pantar (TAP) languages are a western outlier among other Papuan languages, the bulk of which are spoken in and around the island of New Guinea. While the TAP languages constitute a coherent family (Holton et al., 2012; Kaiping and Klamer, 2022), their relationship to other Papuan families of New Guinea has not been demonstrated (Holton and Robinson, 2014; Schapper et al., 2014).

Within the TAP language family dictionaries exist for only a handful of languages, listed here in alphabetical order: Abui (Kratochvíl and Delpada, 2008), Blagar (Steinhauer and Gomang, 2016), Kamang (Schapper and Manimau, 2011), Sawila (Kratochvíl et al., 2014), Teiwa (Klamer, 2012), and Western Pantar (Holton and Koly, 2007). These dictionaries exist in printed form and have been also distributed in the speech community. For the remaining languages a number of wordlists exist: from 1930s the Holle lists (Holle et al., 1980), Stokhof lists (Stokhof, 1975), and various wordlists produced by the Indonesian Language Development and Fostering Agency (Pusat Bahasa Indonesia). All available wordlists are consolidated in the LexiRumah online database (Kaiping et al., 2022) which contains at least two hundred words per language.

None of the above listed TAP dictionaries contain more than 4,000 words although each of them took several years to create. Beyond the basic vocabulary, which is also included in the LexiRumah wordlists, the dictionary coverage is determined by the collected texts and the preferences of the compilers. As a result each dictionary inevitably contains random gaps. The lexicographic workflow in language description is slow, over-reliant on a single author or a small team; it does not produce lexicographic materials suitable for language revitalisation or natural language processing applications. There is generally little concern for "open" data and shared formats.

1.1 Lexicography of low-resource languages

Field linguists use a variety of lexicographic tools. Their main producer is the Summer Institute of Linguistics (SIL) which developed the SIL multi-dictionary format (MDF) described in Coward and Grimes (2000) and utilised it in the following tools:

- SIL Shoebox[1] (1st generation corpus management tool, parser, and dictionary builder)
- SIL Toolbox[2] (2nd generation corpus management tool, parser, and dictionary builder)
- SIL Lexique Pro[3] (2nd generation dictionary management tool)
- SIL FieldWorks[4] (3rd generation, with all previous functionalities, plus automated grammar generation)

[1] https://software.sil.org/shoebox/
[2] https://software.sil.org/toolbox/
[3] https://software.sil.org/lexiquepro/
[4] https://software.sil.org/fieldworks/

Proceedings of the first workshop on NLP applications to field linguistics, pages 54–63
July 5–10, 2020. ©2020 Association for Computational Linguistics
https://doi.org/10.26615/978-954-452-056-4_007

- SIL WeSay[5] (4th generation, a collaborative native-speaker oriented lexicographic tool)
- LanguageForge[6] (a web-based dictionary development tool sharing the data format with FieldWorks but running on any OS with a browser)

In addition, the Max Planck Institute introduced the MPI Lexus online plaform[7] which did not become mainstream. For comparative wordlists the comma-separated-value format is now mainstream and it is used in all Cross-Linguistic Linked Data[8] databases such as Dictionaria[9] or the The Austronesian Comparative Dictionary Online[10].

1.2 Desiderata

Lexicography of low-resource language requires tools with broad functionality. Firstly, the tools should support making fine-grained meaning distinctions (instead of 5 verbs glossed as 'cut' offer means to systematically distinguish them). The tools should also allow the lexicographer to monitor the coverage of various semantic fields to produce balanced resources. Finally, a dictionary should be structured in a way that enables its use in semantic typology.

Next, the tools should complement grammatical description, embedding information on phonetics, morphosyntax, usage, etc., and support semantic tagging of the corpus. The tools should support itegration of the lexicon and corpus, to draw naturalistic examples.

Another concern are the data formats which should rely on the maturing standards in the NLP. The interoperability with such standards is a prerequisite for gaining benefits from existing resources for major languages. For example, when identifying the most appropriate sense of a word in the low-resource language, equivalents in other major languages should be discoverable automatically.

Finally, the lexicographic tools should systematically support crowd-sourcing and community maintenance because it is unlikely that the number of professional linguists studying a low-resource language can ever become adequate for the task at hand.

We believe that wordnets are tools that meet the above desiderata and we will briefly characterise them in the next section.

2 Wordnets and Low-resource Languages

There are two main methods to build wordnets (Vossen, 1998). The first is known as the 'expansion approach', where the semantic hierarchy of another wordnet is used as pivot. In this approach, the required work is essentially a translation effort – conserving the structure of the pivot wordnet and translating individual nodes of the hierarchy, which can be done incrementally (i.e. usually starting by a subset of frequent concepts) but can take in principle infinitely long until all language specific senses are identified. The Princeton Wordnet (PWN, Fellbaum, 1998) is, by far, the most frequently used pivot for projects that employ the 'expansion approach'.

The second method is known as the 'merge approach'. And while this approach is perhaps more principled, in theory, it is both slow and it also requires more resources. In the 'merge approach' no pivot structure is assumed. As such, this method can ensure higher degrees of freedom while modeling the structure of the wordnet without depending on pre-assumed semantic relations. One of the immediate benefits of this approach is the ability to freely add new concepts that are not part of the pivot language – a problem many wordnet projects that followed the 'expansion' approach have struggled with. The major drawback of this approach, however, is its inability to immediately benefit from the parallel translations available from all other projects that used the same pivot.

2.1 The Collaborative Interlingual Index (CILI)

In recent years there have been two major changes to wordnets that have made wordnets more suitable to deal with low-resource languages. These are: the Collaborative Interlingual Index (**CILI**, Bond et al., 2016) and a new and improved Wordnet Lexical Markup Framework (**WN-LMF**, P. McCrae et al., 2021).

CILI has solved the linking problem: before CILI it was necessary to use one language as a pivot to link other languages. Historically, this pivot has been the Princeton WordNet (Fellbaum,

[5] https://software.sil.org/wesay/
[6] https://languageforge.org/
[7] https://www.mpi.nl/corpus/html/lexus/index.html
[8] https://clld.org/
[9] https://dictionaria.clld.org/
[10] https://acd.clld.org/

1998) – a decision embraced by the Open Multilingual Wordnet 1.0 (OMW, Bond and Foster, 2013), a projected that linked dozens of wordnets projects using English as a pivot language. Even though the choice of English as a pivot brought forth many benefits, this quickly became problematic to describe non-main-stream languages whose concept inventories often differ from English (i.e., many languages have senses for concepts that had not been described for English, making it quite difficult to streamline the development of a wordnet that did not largely overlap with English).

As an alternative, instead of chosing English as a pivot, wordnets were developed independently from English, but the downside of such approach is that wordnets can no longer be linked together. The independent construction has historically only been viable for very large projects, with a strong funded agenda, and is not really recommended for smaller projects.[11]

CILI, which was largely inspired by the Interlingual Index (ILI) developed for the EuroWordNet (Vossen, 1998), ended the need to use any specific language as pivot. CILI not only allows any language to contribute to a language-agnostic concept inventory, but also allows a language to link directly to other languages without using English as pivot, harnessing the advances in meaning description made in any linked language.

As an example we may give the Abui word *liik* 'elevated wooden platform' which can refer to a chair, table, a gazebo, wooden house floor, verandah, gallery or a stage and corresponds quite well to the Indonesian and Malay words *balai-balai* or *bale-bale*, which have no simple equivalent in English. English does not have a generic word describing an elevated wooden platform but usually lexicalises its size or purpose. In CILI the Abui and Indonesian/Malay words can be linked without the need to link to English.

There may also be words that are unique for Abui (and perhaps related languages) which have no counterparts in English or Indonesian, but may have one in one of the languages already linked to CILI. Examples of such words are the Abui *neura* 'sibling of the opposite gender' and *nemuknehi* 'sibling of the same gender'. Interestingly, English and Malay lexicalise the gender of the referent while Abui distinguishes the same-gender siblings (brother-brother, and sister-sister *nemuknehi*) from opposite gender (brother-sister = *neura*).

[11]This is discussed in greater detail more in Section 4.

2.2 WN-LMF

The second major breakthrough that now extends the utility of wordnets (for fieldwork or otherwise) is the improved and continuously expanding WN-LMF. Wordnets traditionally contained only open class words (i.e., nouns, verbs, adjectives and adverbs) – which immediately raised limitations on the use of wordnets as fuller lexicons. However, this restriction is no longer true, as can be seen by an increasing trend in expanding wordnets not only to other word classes – e.g., pronouns (Seah and Bond, 2014), exclamatives (Morgado da Costa and Bond, 2016), classifiers (Morgado da Costa et al., 2016) – but also to expand wordnet towards new depths of linguistics analysis, to include new layers of annotation that include better ways to represent regional or diachronic orthographic variation, pronunciation (incl. links to audio files), syntactic modeling, and much more. These efforts are constantly being updated on a need basis, and are summarized in a publicly released WN-LMF schema that strongly encourages different languages to encode this information in a shared format.

2.3 Open Multilingual Wordnet

The Open Multilingual Wordnet (OMW, Bond and Foster, 2013) is, perhaps, the best example of the benefits provided by the 'expansion approach'. The OMW currently links dozens of open wordnets using PWN as the pivot structure. The language alignments provided by all these parallel wordnets are extremely useful for many downstream NLP tasks, such as Machine Translation and Word Sense Disambiguation.

A recent change to the way the OMW operates was introduced with the creation of the Collaborative Interlingual Index (CILI, Bond et al., 2016) – an open, language agnostic, flat-structured index that links wordnets across languages without imposing the hierarchy of any single wordnet. Through CILI, multiple projects are now able to link to each other and to contribute directly to the set of CILI's concepts without the penalty of being frozen within an imposed structure.

Naturally, CILI was initially created using the concept set provided by the PWN (i.e. all PWN concepts have a direct link to CILI), the quickest and easiest way to link a new wordnet to CILI is still to use the expansion approach with PWN's hierarchy as pivot – and this is what we chose to do.

The architecture linking multiple wordnets has been implemented in the Open Multilingual Wordnet (OMW) allowing the low-resource wordnets to be linked and studied so that their properties can inform the future development and design decisions. The authors of OMW make a strong point for unrestricted (u) or attribution required (a) license release (Bond and Foster, 2013).

The new (upcoming) version of the OMW will enforce the use of the WN-LMF, further encouraging the adoption of this schema among existing wordnets, and most certainly also encouraging further discussion on future needs to expand the WN-LMF to accommodate new/missing information.

2.4 Integration of low-resource languages into global wordnet

As described in the beginning of this section, wordnets constructed before the introduction of CILI had to either be developed independently of English (merge approach) or use the PWN as their pivot (expansion approach). An example of the merge-approach is the Yami wordnet whose authors attempted to incorporate elaborate and specific information on certain semantic domains, taking the Yami fish terminology as a test case (Yang et al., 2010). As other examples may serve the Vietnamese wordnet (Lam and Kalita, 2018), Mansi wordnet (Horváth et al., 2016) or the human-curated wordnet of Old-Javanese (Moeljadi and Aminullah, 2020), which has to rely on deep philological knowledge in the absence of native speakers.

The Cantonese wordnet (Sio and Costa, 2019) is an example of the extension approach. It is a high-quality human-curated resource derived from the Chinese Open Wordnet and the PWN.

The extension approach is suitable for automatic methods, as demonstrated by the Shipibo-Konibo wordnet (Maguiño-Valencia et al., 2018) which was derived from Spanish glosses extracted from a 1993 Spanish-Shipibo-Konibo dictionary. The outcome of the automatic linking was manually evaluated.

Our approach is the closest to that taken in the creation of the wordnets for Kristang (Morgado da Costa, 2020) and Coptic (Slaughter et al., 2019) to which we will refer in more detail in section 4.2.

3 Lexicographic resources for Abui

Abui (ISO 639-3: abz, abui1241) is a Timor-Alor-Pantar (TAP) language spoken by about 17 thousand speakers in an area stretching from the northern to the southern coast in Central Alor. Abui is classified by Kaiping and Klamer (2022) to the Central Alor branch of TAP. The work reported here focusses on the variety spoken in the village of Takalelang at the northern coast.

The earliest lexicographic work on Abui comes from the pen of two anthropologists who conducted their research in late 1930s in the Abui village of Atengmelang. Cora Du Bois, who published a monograph on the Abui culture (Bois and Kardiner, 1944), left behind extensive lexical and grammatical notes (part of the Cora Du Bois Personal Papers at the Tozzer Library, Harvard University, [CDBpapers]). Martha Maria Nicolspeyer appended to her PhD thesis an Abui-Dutch wordlist (Nicolspeyer, 1940) [N1940]. This work served as a base for W. A. L. Stokhof, who worked on Abui in late 1970s and 1980s and published the Du Bois wordlists and provided an Abui text with a grammatical commentary (Stokhof, 1975, 1984) [S1975].

Since 2003 the Abui language has been subject to more intensive study which resulted in a full grammatical description (Kratochvíl, 2007) and a dictionary primer (Kratochvíl and Delpada, 2008) [KD2008]. The dictionary is derived from a Toolbox corpus and contains only words which are attested in texts that were recorded during the documentation.

The dictionary was revised and expanded in its second edition (Kratochvíl and Delpada, 2014) [KD2014], available online and counting over 400 pages. It includes Abui-English, Abui-Indonesian and reverses, as well as a semantic ontology based on the SIL semantic domains (Moe, 2013).

Between 2013 and 2016, three Rapid Words workshops were conducted, during which about 17 thousand words [RW2016] were collected using a crowd-sourcing approach designed by the Summer Institute of Linguistics (Boerger and Stutzman, 2018). Currently, these words are being digitised and equiped with their English, Indonesian and Malay glosses before the method described here can be applied. Table 1 offers an overview of the available Abui lexicographic work to date including its size and estimation of the production time (in years). The works are identified by the abbreviations used above.

Author(s)	Type	Words	Years
N1940	dictionary	710	0.5
CDBpapers	wordlist	2063	2
S1975	wordlist	117	n.a.
KD2008	dictionary	1757	4
KD2014	dictionary	2389	6
RW2016	wordlist	>17k	>6

Table 1: Overview of the Abui lexical resources

4 Developing the Abui Wordnet

Building and maintaining a wordnet is extremely time-consuming, especially when this is done manually. For this reason, the large majority of wordnets are built by bootstrapping their development using one or more existing wordnets, referred to as the "pivot languages", as we discussed in section 2. In this section we discuss the methods to build the Abui wordnet.

4.1 Extracting Toolbox Data

The SIL Toolbox dictionaries are based on the Multi-dictionary format (MDF) by Coward and Grimes (2000). The format defines a broad range of fields which are marked by a generic ID starting with a backslash (eg. \lx, \ph, \ps, etc.). MDF is rich and versatile: it incorporates linguistic information (pronunciation, morphosyntactic properties, meaning, examples), cultural information, sources (e.g. books, narratives, speakers), etc. An example of a lemma can be seen in Figure 1 which contains the Abui verb *pok* 'split, burst'. The figure consists of two blocks. The left block in sans-serif case contains the data from the Abui dictionary. The right column and the shading is our own and separates the lemma fields into blocks and characterises their content.

The first field of each entry is a lemma (\lx), which is followed by its pronunciation (\ph) and part-of-speech (\ps). The meaning is captured by a gloss, reverse gloss, and definition in English (\ge, \re, \de), Indonesian (\gn, etc.), and Alor Malay (\gr, etc.) Finally, the entry also contains an example sentence and its translations in English, Indonesian and Malay.

Figure 1 shows that there is some redundancy in the MDF format. For example the information in the gloss field (\ge, \gn, \gr) is always repeated in the reversal field (\re, \rn, \rr). The definition field (\de, \dn, \dr) may occasionally contains more information than the gloss and the reversal, as it

```
\lx pok                                   ⇐ lemma
\ph 'pɔk                                  ⇐ pronunciation
\ps v.0
\pn kki                                   ⇐ part of speech
\ge split                                 ⇐ gloss, reversal,
\re broken                                  and definition (ENG)
\re smashed
\re split
\de split, burst, hatch, broken, smashed
\gn pecah
\rn retak                                 ⇐ gloss, reversal,
\rn menetas                                 and definition (IND)
\rn pecah
\dn pecah, menetas, retak
\gr peca                                  ⇐ gloss, reversal,
\rr menetas                                 and definition (MLZ)
\rr peca
\dr peca, menetas
\ref Poku.001                             ⇐ example sentence
\xv Pingai nu hayei poku.                   and translations
\xe A plate fell down and broke.
\xn Piring itu jatuh dan pecah.
\xr Piring tu jatu peca.
```

Figure 1: The lemma for *pok* 'split, burst' (MDF format)

Abui Lemmas	2,508
English Lemmas	4,985
English Definitions	2,766
Indonesian Lemmas	3,829
Indonesian Definitions	5,771
Malay Lemmas	3,267
Malay Definitions	2,633

Table 2: Summary of data extracted from Toolbox

is the case also in the lemma for *pok* 'split, burst' above.

For the work presented in this paper, we used only the information contained in the Abui lemma, part-of-speech, reverse glosses (referred as individual language lemmas) and definitions. Table 2 provides a summary of the amount of information extracted from the Abui Toolbox dictionary.

The table reveals that the number of Indonesian definitions is higher than the number of lexemes because different senses of the word were included under the same lexeme, such as *aha* for which three senses were listed: (i) 'outside', (ii) 'outside, in the fields' and (iii) 'blade, the sharp part of a cutting tool'. Each sense contains a separate definition, but the reverse glosses for Indonesian are shared across all available senses.

4.2 Multilingual Sense Intersection

In our work, we exploit the existing lexicographic work on Abui to bootstrap the development of the wordnet following the expansion approach while acquiring sense candidates through a naive algorithm inspired by multilingual sense intersection (Bonansinga and Bond, 2016; Bond and Bonansinga, 2015) to determine potential senses of a new wordnet – a similar method to the one employed to build Coptic Wordnet (Slaughter et al., 2019), while using field data instead of dictionary data.

Multilingual sense intersection has a simple logical foundation. The base idea is that the semantic space of a polysemous word in any language can be constrained by aligned translations of the same word in other languages. This same concept has been used in automatic Word Sense Disambiguation (WSD) using parallel text. And using data with an increasing number parallel languages has been shown to incrementally improve the sense disambiguation. In our case, however, instead of using parallel text to disambiguate multiple languages at the same time, we use existing wordnets as pivots to generate candidate senses for a new wordnet. Figure 2 shows a conceptualization of this logic, for three languages.

We used available wordnet data for the three languages present in our Toolbox data – English, Indonesian and Alor Malay (a Vehicular Malay variety). English wordnet data came primarily from the Princeton Wordnet (Fellbaum, 1998). Indonesian and Malay data came primarily from Wordnet Bahasa (Noor et al., 2011; Bond et al., 2014).

In addition to these wordnets, we used data made available by the Extended Open Multilingual Wordnet (Bond and Foster, 2013), which contains automatically collected data from Wiktionary and the Unicode Common Locale Data Repository (CLDR), as well as data made available through the ongoing sense annotation efforts of the NTU Multilingual Corpus (Tan and Bond, 2014; Bond et al., 2021) – which have expanded the sense inventory of the above mentioned wordnets.

Figure 2 illustrates a hypothetical scenario where a single Abui lemma is a candidate sense for nine possible concepts (*concept.1–9*). However, these nine senses are not all equally suggested by the three languages. In this example, the available English (ENG) translations suggest five concepts, the Indonesian (IND) translations also suggest five concepts (although not the same five), and the Malay (ZSM) translations suggest three concepts.

A natural way to organize this data is by the number of languages that suggest any given sense.

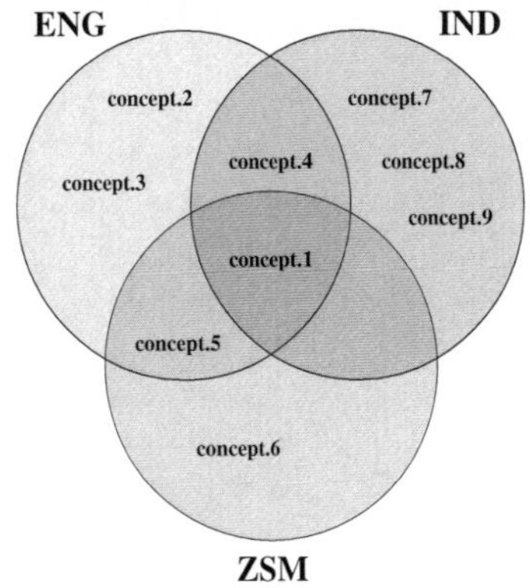

Figure 2: Sense Intersection visualisation: coloured circles represent lexemes which refer to a number of senses (concept.1-9). Unrelated languages are less likely to colexicalise the same set of senses.

In our example, *concept.1* would be suggested by all three languages, while both *concept.4* and *concept.5* would be suggested by alignments in only two languages. Empirically, it is easy to understand that senses suggested by more languages have a higher likelihood of being correct.

In addition to determining the number of intersected languages, our current algorithm also uses other simple metrics to rank Abui sense candidates, including: number of individual senses matched within a concept for each language (each worth ten points); and the number of matches between an existing wordnet sense and the definition extracted through Toolbox (each worth one point).

Since most synsets in wordnet have more than one sense, the ranking score in our algorithm seeks to reward candidates that show a greater overlap with the information contained in each wordnet. This means, for example, that the Princeton Wordnet concept for the verb `00056930-v (cause to be born)`, which has five difference senses (*bear; have; birth; deliver; give birth*), would contribute with a score of ten points for each lemma that was included in the English translations of Abui Toolbox dictionary entry for the corresponding verb. Scores gathered by each language are summed into a final score.

In order to reduce spurious candidates, only data with congruent parts-of-speech (between the wordnets and the Toolbox data) was used. This was done by creating a hand mapping between the fine-grained parts-of-speech labels included in the Toolbox dictionary, and the simpler tags that used in wordnets.

4.3 Results

The results of our sense intersection experiment are summarized in Tables 3 and 4. Table 3 shows the results in relation to the number of languages that were intersected for each sense candidate. As it would be expected, three-way intersection happens much less frequently than two-way intersection or than senses suggested by a single language. We hand-checked all 2,368 candidate senses suggested by the intersection of three languages. In addition, for candidates informed by either two or one language, we performed a stratified sampling (based on score bands shown in Table 4) and checked an extra 1,200 candidate senses. From this evaluation, we can show that senses suggested by three languages were correct around 99% (0.989) of the time, followed by 50% accuracy for senses suggested by two languages, and 35% of the time for senses suggested by a single language.

These results are in line with those reported by Slaughter et al. (2019), for the Coptic Wordnet, where senses triangulated by three languages were shown to be correct as high as 98% of the time. Our findings are also in line with other similar work, such as Bond and Ogura (2008), who found scores of about 97% when aligning lexicons with three languages.

Table 4 shows a more detailed picture of our sense intersection experiment. It shows results filtered for different language pairings (for the case of two-way intersection), and also filtered by difference score bands for the same type of intersection. The scoring method was briefly described in Section 4.2.

One interesting aspect shown in Table 4 is the fact that two-way language intersection was comparable across all language pairs. Given the proximity between Indonesian and Malay, one would expect that intersection of English with one of the two other languages would result in better sense candidates – but this was not the case. Table 4 also shows that the naive scoring algorithm that expanded the simple metric of number of intersected languages reported in Slaughter et al. (2019) is useful enough to differentiate between candidates that received the same broad triangulation type. Candidates with higher scores in the same intersection type are correct more often. These differences become increasingly relevant the fewer the languages that inform that sense candidate. For senses suggested by a single language, we can see that higher ranking

Intersection	Cand.	Sample	Acc.
3 languages	2,368	2,368	0.99
2 languages	8,115	600	0.50
1 language	28,678	600	0.35

Table 3: Summary of results filtered by number of intersected languages

Intersection	Cand.	Score	Samp.	Acc.
eng+ind	3,032	31-61	100	0.61
eng+ind		20	100	0.34
eng+zsm	206	21-31	60	0.65
eng+zsm		20	140	0.44
ind+zsm	4,877	31-63	100	0.61
ind+zsm		20	100	0.42
eng	9,716	20-32	100	0.67
eng		10	100	0.07
ind	17,380	21-32	100	0.57
ind		10	100	0.11
zsm	1,582	11-21	100	0.44
zsm		10	100	0.22

Table 4: Summary of results for one and two-way intersection filtered by languages and ranking score

scores (which reflect that more than one sense in that language was match for a single concept) can be extremely useful to discern likely candidates. In our data, the most extreme case can be seen for English, where senses presenting a ranking score of 10 (i.e., informed by a single English sense) have an average accuracy of 7% but senses with a score between 20 and 32 (informed by more than one English sense) have an average accuracy score of 67%.

These results show that even though our ranking algorithm is very naive, we are moving in the right direction. It would most certainly be beneficial to improve our ranking algorithm with other classic features used in Word Sense Disambiguation, such as exploiting the semantic hierarchy or using wordnet glosses and definitions.

5 Release and Licensing

A summary of the size and part-of-speech coverage of the first release of the Abui Wordnet is given in Table 5. This first release includes only data derived from candidates generated by three-way intersection – which we showed yielded data with a confidence score of 99%. Since all candidates intersected by three languages were hand-checked, we include only those that were confirmed. In addition, compatible morphological alternations were added, semi-automatically (using Toolbox data) to each sense. This increased the number of available senses considerably.

Note the low number of adjectives (which include quantifiers) and adverbs in Table 5, which is a consequence of Abui having just a handful of adjectives and encoding other properties as stative verbs, and similarly expressing event properties mostly by finite verbs (Kratochvíl, 2007, 109-110).

POS	No. Synsets	No. Senses
nouns	818	1,466
verbs	590	2,013
adjective	46	82
adverb	21	45
Total	1,475	3,606

Table 5: Abui Wordnet Coverage (v1.0)

One key motivation for this project was to inspire other field linguistics to follow on our footsteps and release their data using open licenses. Field linguists have a responsibility towards the communities they work with, and should embrace an open-shared ownership of the work that is developed with the help of these communities.

We want to encourage other field linguistics to use and replicate our work, while working towards the maintenance and preservation of Abui and its community. For this reason, the Abui Wordnet is released under a Creative Commons Attribution 4.0 International License (CC BY 4.0)[12]. We have produced OMW tsv files, which can also be used in the Python Natural Language Toolkit (Bird et al., 2009). In addition, and keeping up with the recent requirements to belong to the OMW, we will also release this data using the WN-LMF format[13].

The Abui Wordnet data will be made available on GitHub at `https://github.com/fanacek/abuiwn`.

6 Discussion and Future Work

We have sketched a procedure that facilitates the transfer of the Toolbox MDF-formatted data into a wordnet. And we have also shown that it is possible to generate very high quality data through a naive algorithm based on sense intersection.

We believe our results could be improved further by improving our sense intersection algorithm to include, for example, semantic domain information,[14] or by attempting to exploit other available information often used in the task of Word Sense Disambiguation such as wordnets' semantic hierarchy, glosses and definitions.

In addition, we would like to work towards including pronunciation, grammatical information (aspectual class, valency, etymology and borrowings) and example sentences, all of which we track in the Abui Toolbox dictionary, and which can be accommodated by the Wordnet Lexical Markup Framework (**WN-LMF**, P. McCrae et al., 2021).

In the near future we also expect to have to deal with many specific features particular to Abui: (i) concepts unique to Abui or the region; (ii) extensive specific taxonomy for animals and plants[15]; (iii) many non-lexicalised CILI concepts in Abui (especially linked to technology and modernity).

Finally, another challenge we would like to work on relates to the fact that there is no official Abui orthography and many writing conventions exist which reflect dialectal and idiolectal variation as well as individual preferences regarding the spelling of vowel length, velars and uvulars, tone, and clitics. We are taking an aggregating approach and register all examples of alternative spelling and link them to the respective lemma. In the future we would like to use the full extent of the WN-LMF to make this information available in our wordnet.

7 Conclusion

This paper shows the viability of the intersection method in rapid building of wordnets for low-resource languages using data collected in field linguistics. Applying a similar method as Slaughter et al. (2019) we have reached a overall accuracy of 99% when the sense is defined by the intersection of three languages. The accuracy however does drop steeply when fewer than three languages are available.

[12]https://creativecommons.org/licenses/by/4.0/

[13]https://github.com/globalwordnet/schemas

[14]Semantic domains (`http://semdom.org/`) is an ontology organised in an associative way, grouping words used to talk about an area together, regardless of the subtle differences among them. For example, the English domain Rain includes words such as *rain*, *drizzle*, *downpour*, *raindrop*, *puddle*. The ontology tracks both collocations, as well as paradigm forms such as synonyms, antonyms, generic and specific relations. For example, *fly* will contain a reference to *bird* as a prototypical agent of that event. While *bird* is a generic term *chicken* is more specific.

[15]Blake, A.L. 2018. Documenting environmental knowledge in Abui, a language of eastern Indonesia. London: SOAS University of London, Endangered Languages Archive. `https://www.elararchive.org/dk0574`.

Acknowledgements

The authors acknowledges the generous support of the Czech Science Foundation grant 20-18407S Verb Class Analysis Accelerator for Low- Resource Languages - RoboCorp (PI Kratochvíl) and the EU's Horizon 2020 Marie Skłodowska-Curie grant H2020-MSCA-IF-2020 CHILL – No.101028782 (PI Morgado da Costa).

References

Steven Bird, Ewan Klein, and Edward Loper. 2009. *Natural language processing with Python: Analyzing text with the Natural Language Toolkit NLTK*. O'Reilly Media, Inc.

Brenda H. Boerger and Verna Stutzman. 2018. Single-event rapid word collection workshops: Efficient, effective, empowering. *Language Documentation & Conservation*, 12:147–193.

Cora Alice Du Bois and Abram Kardiner. 1944. *The people of Alor; a social-psychological study of an East Indian Island*. Univ. of Minnesota Press, Minneapolis,. With analyses by Abram Kardiner and Emil Oberholzer. ill.

Giulia Bonansinga and Francis Bond. 2016. Multilingual sense intersection in a parallel corpus with diverse language families. In *Proc. of the 8th Global WordNet Conference*, pages 44–49.

Francis Bond and Giulia Bonansinga. 2015. Exploring cross-lingual sense mapping in a multilingual parallel corpus. In *Proceedings of the Second Italian Conference on Computational Linguistics CLiC-it 2015*, pages 56–61, Trento.

Francis Bond and Ryan Foster. 2013. Linking and extending an open multilingual Wordnet. In *Proceedings of the 51st Annual Meeting of the Association for Computational Linguistics (Volume 1: Long Papers)*, pages 1352–1362, Sofia, Bulgaria. Association for Computational Linguistics.

Francis Bond, Andrew Kirkrose Devadason, Rui Lin Melissa Teo, and Luis Morgado Da Costa. 2021. Teaching through tagging — interactive lexical semantics. In *Proceedings of the 11th Global WordNet Conference (GWC 2021)*, Pretoria, South Africa. Global Wordnet Association.

Francis Bond, Lian Tze Lim, Enya Kong Tang, and Hammam Riza. 2014. The combined wordnet bahasa. *NUSA: Linguistic studies of languages in and around Indonesia*, (57):83–100.

Francis Bond and Kentaro Ogura. 2008. Combining linguistic resources to create a machine-tractable Japanese-Malay dictionary. *Language Resources and Evaluation*, 42(2):127–136.

Francis Bond, Piek Vossen, John P McCrae, and Christiane Fellbaum. 2016. Cili: the collaborative interlingual index. In *Proceedings of the Global WordNet Conference*, volume 2016.

David F Coward and Charles E Grimes. 2000. *A guide to lexicography and the Multi-Dictionary Formatter*. SIL International, Waxhaw, North Carolina.

Christiane Fellbaum, editor. 1998. *WordNet: An Electronic Lexical Database*. MIT Press, Cambridge, MA.

K. F Holle, W. A. L Stokhof, Lia Saleh-Bronkhorst, and Alma E Almanar. 1980. *Holle lists: vocabularies in languages of Indonesia*. Dept. of Linguistics, Research School of Pacific Studies, Australian National University, Canberra.

Gary Holton, Marian Klamer, František Kratochvíl, Laura C. Robinson, and Antoinette Schapper. 2012. The Historical Relations of the Papuan Languages of Alor and Pantar. *Oceanic Linguistics*, 51(1):86–122.

Gary Holton and Mahalalel Lamma Koly. 2007. *Kamus Pengantar Bahasa Pantar Barat: Tubbe - Mauta - Lamma*.

Gary Holton and Laura C. Robinson. 2014. The Linguistic Position of the Timor-Alor-Pantar Languages. In Marian Klamer, editor, *The Alor-Pantar Languages: History and Typology*, pages 155–198. Language Science Press, Berlin.

Csilla Horváth, Ágoston Nagy, Norbert Szilágyi, and Veronika Vincze. 2016. Where bears have the eyes of currant: Towards a Mansi WordNet. In *Proceedings of the 8th Global WordNet Conference (GWC)*, pages 131–135, Bucharest, Romania. Global Wordnet Association.

Gereon A. Kaiping, Owen Edwards, and Marian Klamer. Lexirumah 3.0.0 [online]. 2022.

Gereon A. Kaiping and Marian Klamer. 2022. The dialect chain of the Timor-Alor-Pantar language family: A new analysis using systematic Bayesian phylogenetics. *Language Dynamics and Change*, 12(2):274 – 326.

Marian Klamer. 2012. *Kosa kata Bahasa Teiwa-Indonesia-Inggris (Teiwa-Indonesian-English glossary)*. Language and Culture Unit UBB, Kupang.

František Kratochvíl, Isak Bantara, and Anderias Malaikosa. 2014. Sawila-English dictionary. Ms.

František Kratochvíl and Benidiktus Delpada. 2008. *Kamus Pengantar Bahasa Abui: Abui – Indonesian – English Dictionary*. UBB-GMIT, Kupang, Indonesia.

František Kratochvíl and Benidiktus Delpada. 2014. Abui-English-Indonesian Dictionary. 2nd. edition.

František Kratochvíl. 2007. *A grammar of Abui: a Papuan language of Alor*. LOT, Utrecht.

Khang Nhut Lam and Jugal Kalita. 2018. Constructing vietnamese wordnet: A case study. In *19th International Conference on Computational Linguistics and Intelligent Text Processing, March 18 to 24, 2018, Hanoi, Vietnam.*

Diego Maguiño-Valencia, Arturo Oncevay-Marcos, and Marco A. Sobrevilla Cabezudo. 2018. WordNet-shp: Towards the building of a lexical database for a Peruvian minority language. In *Proceedings of the Eleventh International Conference on Language Resources and Evaluation (LREC 2018)*, Miyazaki, Japan. European Language Resources Association (ELRA).

Ron Moe. 2013. Semantic domains. `http://semdom.org`. (Accessed 2022-08-01).

David Moeljadi and Zakariya Pamuji Aminullah. 2020. Building the old Javanese Wordnet. In *Proceedings of the 12th Language Resources and Evaluation Conference*, pages 2940–2946, Marseille, France. European Language Resources Association.

Luis Morgado da Costa. 2020. Pinchah Kristang: A dictionary of kristang. In *Proceedings of the Globalex2020 at the 12th Edition of the Language Resources and Evaluation Conference*, Marseille, France. European Language Resources Association (ELRA).

Luís Morgado da Costa and Francis Bond. 2016. Wow! What a useful extension! Introducing non-referential concepts to WordNet. In *Proceedings of the 10th edition of the International Conference on Language Resources and Evaluation (LREC 2016)*, pages 4323–4328, Portorož, Slovenia.

Luís Morgado da Costa, Francis Bond, and Helena Gao. 2016. Mapping and generating classifiers using an open chinese ontology. In *Proceedings of the 8th Global WordNet Conference (GWC 2016)*, Bucharest, Romania.

Martha Margaretha Nicolspeyer. 1940. *De sociale structuur van een Aloreesche bevolkingsgroep*. V. A. Kramers, Rijswijk (Z.-H.).

Nurril Hirfana Bte Mohamed Noor, Suerya Sapuan, and Francis Bond. 2011. Creating the open wordnet bahasa. In *Proceedings of the 25th Pacific Asia Conference on Language, Information and Computation*, pages 255–264.

John P. McCrae, Michael Wayne Goodman, Francis Bond, Alexandre Rademaker, Ewa Rudnicka, and Luis Morgado Da Costa. 2021. The GlobalWordNet formats: Updates for 2020. In *Proceedings of the 11th Global WordNet Conference (GWC 2021)*, Pretoria, South Africa. Global Wordnet Association.

Muhammad Zulhelmy bin Mohd Rosman, František Kratochvíl, and Francis Bond. 2014. Bringing together over- and under- represented languages: Linking WordNet to the SIL Semantic Domains. In *Proceedings of the Seventh Global Wordnet Conference*, pages 40–48, Tartu, Estonia. University of Tartu Press.

Antoinette Schapper, Juliette Huber, and Aone van Engelenhoven. 2014. The relatedness of Timor-Kisar and Alor-Pantar languages: A preliminary demonstration. In Marian Klamer, editor, *Alor-Pantar languages: History and typology*, pages 99–154. Language Science Press, Berlin.

Antoinette Schapper and Marten Manimau. 2011. *Kamus Pengantar Bahasa Kamang-Indonesia-Inggris: Introductory Kamang-Indonesian-English Dictionary*. Unit Bahasa Dan Budaya, Kupang.

Yu Jie Seah and Francis Bond. 2014. Annotation of pronouns in a multilingual corpus of Mandarin Chinese, English and Japanese. In *Proceedings 10th Joint ISO-ACL SIGSEM Workshop on Interoperable Semantic Annotation*, pages 82–88.

Joanna Ut-Seong Sio and Luis Morgado Da Costa. 2019. Building the Cantonese Wordnet. In *Proceedings of the 10th Global Wordnet Conference*, pages 206–215, Wroclaw, Poland. Global Wordnet Association.

Laura Slaughter, Luis Morgado Da Costa, So Miyagawa, Marco Büchler, Amir Zeldes, Hugo Lundhaug, and Heike Behlmer. 2019. The Making of Coptic Wordnet. In *Proceedings of the 10th Global WordNet Conference (GWC 2019)*, Wroclaw, Poland.

Hein Steinhauer and Hendrik D. R. Gomang. 2016. *Kamus Blagar-Indonesia-Inggris / Blagar-Indonesian-English Dictionary*. Yayasan Pustaka Obor Indonesia, Jakarta.

W. A. L Stokhof. 1975. *Preliminary notes on the Alor and Pantar languages (East Indonesia)*. Pacific linguistics. Series B. Dept. of Linguistics, Research School of Pacific Studies, Australian National University, Canberra. By W. A. L. Stokhof. maps ; 26 cm.

W. A. L Stokhof. 1984. Annotations to a text in the Abui language (Alor). *Bijdragen tot de taal-, land- en volkenkunde*, 140(1):106–162.

Liling Tan and Francis Bond. 2014. NTU-MC toolkit: Annotating a linguistically diverse corpus. In *Proceedings of COLING 2014, the 25th International Conference on Computational Linguistics: System Demonstrations*, pages 86–89.

Piek Vossen. 1998. A multilingual database with lexical semantic networks. *Dordrecht: Kluwer Academic Publishers. doi*, 10:978–94.

Meng-Chien Yang, D Victoria Rau, and Ann Hui-Huan Chang. 2010. A proposed model for constructing a Yami wordnet. In *2010 International Conference on Asian Language Processing*, pages 289–292. IEEE.

How to encode arbitrarily complex morphology in word embeddings, no corpus needed

Lane Schwartz
Department of Computer Science
University of Alaska Fairbanks
lane.schwartz@alaska.edu

Coleman Haley
Institute for Language, Cognition and Computation
University of Edinburgh
Coleman.Haley@ed.ac.uk

Francis Tyers
Department of Linguistics
Indiana University
ftyers@iu.edu

Abstract

In this paper, we present a straightforward technique for constructing interpretable word embeddings from morphologically analyzed examples (such as interlinear glosses) for all of the world's languages. Currently, fewer than 300–400 languages out of approximately 7000 have have more than a trivial amount of digitized texts; of those, between 100–200 languages (most in the Indo-European language family) have enough text data for BERT embeddings of reasonable quality to be trained. The word embeddings in this paper are explicitly designed to be both linguistically interpretable and fully capable of handling the broad variety found in the world's diverse set of 7000 languages, regardless of corpus size or morphological characteristics. We demonstrate the applicability of our representation through examples drawn from a typologically diverse set of languages whose morphology includes prefixes, suffixes, infixes, circumfixes, templatic morphemes, derivational morphemes, inflectional morphemes, and reduplication.

1 Better representations are needed

The past several years have seen the development of neural techniques capable of creating extremely high quality word embeddings, most notably BERT (Devlin et al., 2019) and its many variants. In total, however, fewer than 300–400 languages have have more than a trivial amount of digitized text data, thus rendering data-driven NLP approaches including BERT futile for more than 6000 remaining languages (representing over 1.2 billion people; Vannini and Crosnier, 2012; Joshi et al., 2020), even with aggressive multilingual models, transfer learning, bilingual anchoring, and typologically-aware modelling (Ponti et al., 2019; Michel et al., 2020; Eder et al., 2021; Hedderich et al., 2021).

Somewhere between 100–200 languages (most in the Indo-European language family) have enough digitized text data (Joshi et al., 2020; Conneau et al., 2020) for BERT embeddings of reasonable quality to be trained using a combination of techniques including unsupervised sub-word segmentation methods, multilingual bootstrapping, and transfer learning. Quality of word embeddings is substantially lower when corpus sizes are insufficiently large; Alabi et al. (2020), for example, constructed word embeddings using approximately 10 million tokens for Yorùbá[1] and Twi,[2] and found that the resulting embeddings are substantially poorer in quality those for high-resource languages.

1.1 Complex morphology is the norm

The issue of insufficient training data is exacerbated even more when productive derivational and inflectional morphology plays a significant role in word formation in a language. The average number of morphemes per word is medium or high for the vast majority of the world's approximately 7000 languages (see *World Atlas of Language Structures*, including Bickel and Nichols, 2013; Dryer, 2013). Despite this fact, since at least Oettinger (1954), the primary meaning-bearing unit used to represent language in natural language models has been the word.

While many modern NLP models can and sometimes do represent higher-level linguistics units (representing phrases, clauses, or sentences) and lower-level linguistic units (such as morphemes, sub-word chunks, or characters), and notwithstanding the widespread use of unsupervised subword

[1]ISO 639-3: *yor*, an analytic language in the Yoruboid branch of the Niger-Congo language family

[2]ISO 639-3: *twi*, an analytic language in the Tano branch of the Niger-Congo language family

Proceedings of the first workshop on NLP applications to field linguistics, pages 64–76
July 5–10, 2020. ©2020 Association for Computational Linguistics
https://doi.org/10.26615/978-954-452-056-4_008

segmentation methods (BPE, SentencePiece, etc), there remains a very common yet rarely stated assumption that the word should be treated as the primary meaning-bearing unit of language. This assumption likely stems from the historical and current dominance of English[3] as the language of study in NLP (Bender, 2011; Joshi et al., 2020), and the fact that in English, many words do in fact consist of only a single morpheme. English and Standard Mandarin Chinese[4] are prime examples of analytical languages where the average number of morphemes per word is low and for which existing neural representations such as BERT work very well (Peters et al., 2018; Devlin et al., 2019; Zhang et al., 2019).

1.2 Novel Contributions

Existing neural representations are insufficient (§1) for the thousands of languages which lack corpora. In this work, we take up this challenge,[5] surveying existing NLP methods for representing words (§2) and presenting a robust technique (§3) for constructing interpretable word embeddings from morphologically analyzed examples (such as interlinear glosses) for all of the world's languages, even when no corpus exists, and show how linguistic information encoded in these vectors can be successfully recovered.

As the primary contribution of this work, we present extensive proof-of-concept of our model gracefully handling immense morphological variety and hierarchical linguistic structures using complex examples that include concatenation and zero inflection (§4.1), circumfixation (§4.2), fusion (§4.3), polysynthesis (§4.4), agglutination (§4.5), infixation (§4.6), reduplication (§4.7), and templatic morphology (§4.8).

2 Existing Word Representations are Insufficient for Most Languages

Computational processing of natural language requires practical digital representations of the words of a language. We survey existing methods for representing words, arguing that while existing word representations work well for high resource analytic languages like English, existing representations are insufficient for effectively representing morphologically complex words in thousands of languages for which large corpora do not exist.

2.1 Representing characters as integers

Oettinger (1954, ch. 2, p. 11), in the very first Ph.D. granted in the field of NLP, defined a word as "any string of letters preceded and followed by a space or a punctuation mark," and stored each word in an electronic dictionary as a sequence of characters, with each character represented digitally as a 5-bit integer. Nearly seventy years later, with relatively minor variations, this definition is still widely used in the NLP research community. Most digital word representations incorporate this technique, storing each character (or Unicode codepoint, as Clark et al., 2022, do) in a word as a multi-bit integer.

2.2 Representing words as feature bundles

During the 1960s through the early 1990s, most NLP systems utilized a knowledge-based paradigm in which words were represented as complex bundles of linguistic features, which were subsequently processed using linguistically-motivated rules (Hutchins, 1986). Finite-state morphological analyzers (Beesley and Karttunen, 2003) can be used to segment words into sequences of component morphemes; such segmentations can include explicit linguistic features such as case, number, and mood in addition to morpheme identity. Another modern example of this type of linguistically feature-rich word representation can be seen in the attribute-value matrices (AVMs) of Head-driven Phrase Structure Grammars (HPSG; Pollard and Sag, 1994). Such linguistically-based feature bundle representations can in principle work with any language, regardless of corpus size or morphological characteristics, but must be constructed by an expert linguist for each language, and do not naturally fit with many existing neural techniques.

2.3 Representing words as integers

The development of large digital corpora (primarily in English) and the rise of empirical approaches to NLP in the late 1980s and early 1990s, led to widespread use of statistical language models and translation models (see Church and Mercer, 1993; Manning and Schütze, 1999; Koehn, 2010). When implementing these statistical models, it is often convenient to map each word type to an integer,

[3]ISO 639-3: *eng*, an analytic language in the Germanic branch of the Indo-European language family

[4]ISO 639-3: *cmn*, an analytic language in the Sinitic branch of the Sino-Tibetan language family

[5]"It is better to address the core scientific challenges than to continue to look for easy pickings that are no longer there." (Church, 2011)

allowing these integer word representations to directly serve as indices into probability tables (see for example §5 of Brown et al., 1993). A special integer value (often zero) is typically reserved to represent all words not seen during training.

While representing words as integers is efficient in its use of RAM, it suffers from a serious shortcoming first observed by Bull et al. (1955), namely that no semantic, syntactic, or morphological information is encoded in the word representation (for example, *dog* and *dogs* are treated as completely unrelated word types). This problem is seriously exacerbated in languages with rich morphology, as productive derivational and inflectional morphology may result in extremely large numbers of closely-related word types, few of which are likely to appear in corpora. Schwartz et al. (2020a), for example, found that in one polysynthetic language, approximately every other word in running text will have never been previously seen.

2.4 Representing subwords as integers

Unsupervised techniques can be used to automatically segment words into sequences of shorter subword tokens generally longer than the character but shorter than the word. These techniques include approaches such as Morfessor (Creutz and Lagus, 2002; Smit et al., 2014) designed to segment words into units approximating morphemes, and compression-based subword segmentation techniques such as BPE (Sennrich et al., 2016; Wu et al., 2016; Kudo and Richardson, 2018). Most neural NLP systems in broad use today utilize integer representations of unsupervised subword tokens for both input and output.

This approach is more successful at representing words in languages with highly productive morphology than the integer word representations described in §2.3. When corpus sizes are small or nonexistent, however, as is the case for most of the world's languages, insufficient training signal exists to reliably train high-quality unsupervised subword segmentation. This problem can be mitigated through the use of a linguistically-based finite-state morphological analyzer (§2.2) for word segmentation instead of unsupervised segmentation methods (Park et al., 2021).

2.5 Representing (word or subword) types as embeddings

Distributed representations (Hinton et al., 1986), also called continuous representations and word embeddings, represent each word as a point embedded in a high-dimensional vector space. When feed-forward or recurrent neural networks are trained as language models with the task of predicting the next element in a word sequence or a subword sequence, a side effect of the training process is a table of embeddings which can be indexed by the integer representation corresponding to each word (§2.3) or subword (§2.4) type. Other techniques for learning context-independent vector representations for each type include word2vec (Mikolov et al., 2013a) and GloVe (Pennington et al., 2014).

2.6 Representing (word or subword) tokens as embeddings

More recent neural techniques such as ELMo (Peters et al., 2018), BERT (Devlin et al., 2019), and Canine (Clark et al., 2022) can be used to obtain a context-dependent vector representation for each word or subword token. ELMo uses convolutional techniques to generalize over character sequences within the word in conjunction with deep bidirectional recurrent neural networks, while BERT utilizes unsupervised subword tokenization techniques (§2.4) in conjunction with a transformer architecture (Vaswani et al., 2017). Canine treats Unicode codepoints as the subword unit.

Learned context-free word embeddings empirically appear to implicitly encode at least some syntactic and semantic information (Mikolov et al., 2013b). Substantial recent work, summarized by Rogers et al. (2020) indicates that contextualized word embeddings learned by BERT are even more successful at implicitly encoding syntactic, semantic, and possibly morphological information. Interpretability of these embeddings is a challenging problem which is far from solved.

While multilingual training, transfer, and anchoring methods have been shown in some cases to somewhat improve the quality of very low-resource word embeddings over monolingually-trained low-resource word embeddings (see, for example, Eder et al., 2021), such methods rely on digitized monolingual and bilingual resources that exist for only a few hundred languages. It remains the case that at present, training high quality word embeddings is dependent on the availability of large corpora (Alabi et al., 2020; Joshi et al., 2020; Wu and Dredze, 2020; Budur et al., 2020; Michel et al., 2020) consisting of tens or hundreds of millions of tokens, which are available for at most a few hundred languages (see §1).

2.7 Linguistically-informed word embeddings

No existing word representation is capable of robustly representing words in all of the world's languages regardless of corpus size and morphological characteristics. The existing representation that comes closest to meeting these needs is Linguistically Informed Multi-Task BERT (LIMIT-BERT Zhou et al., 2020b), a semi-supervised approach in which a trained parser (Zhou et al., 2020a) is used to annotate large unlabelled corpora. During LIMIT-BERT training, these silver linguistic annotations (part-of-speech tags, constituency trees, and dependency trees) are used along with the words themselves to train contextualized embeddings on five parsing-related tasks.

Unlike the embeddings learned by LIMIT-BERT, the representations we propose are explicitly interpretable by design, allowing for direct recovery of any linguistic features encoded in our word embeddings. Unlike LIMIT-BERT, our approach can produce high-quality word embeddings in the presence of arbitrarily complex morphology and in the absence of a corpus.

3 Embedding and retrieving rich linguistic information

As established in §1, there are thousands of languages which lack the large corpora needed for reliably training neural language models such as BERT. For many of these cases, the size of corpora may be very small or even nonexistent. While multilingual and bootstrapping approaches certainly have a role to play, we ought not ignore the rich linguistic information embedded in morphological analyses.

Essentially every language that is even partly documented has numerous such analyses in the form of interlinear glossed text (ILGs) created by expert linguists. Instead of relying on neural networks to induce linguistic patterns by processing massive corpora, we argue that for more than 6000 so-called "low-resource" languages, a more fruitful method for initializing meaningful word and subword embeddings is by directly embedding the rich linguistic information included in the morphological analyses found in ILGs and (when they exist) other morphologically analyzed corpora.

3.1 Word Embedding Desiderata

We argue that the following desiderata are necessary in order to fulfill the use case of establishing meaningful word embeddings for all languages, even in the absence of any corpus. The representation must easily model words from polysynthetic languages, agglutinative languages, fusional languages, and isolating languages equally well, naturally incorporating any and all linguistic features which may be present in an interlinear gloss or available from other external resources. The representation must model words in ultra-low-resource settings where corpus sizes are very small or even non-existent just as well as it handles words in high-resource settings with very large corpora. Finally, the representation must be interpretable; all linguistic features encoded in the resulting word embeddings should easily retrievable from the word embeddings.

3.2 Tensor Product Representation

To satisfy the word representation desiderata specified in §3.1, we utilize the Tensor Product Representation (TPR) proposed by Smolensky (1990). The use of TPRs provides a principled way of representing hierarchical symbolic information from external resources such as interlinear glosses or morphological analyzers into vector spaces, such as those used as the input and output domains of neural networks. The nature of TPRs enable simple linear algebra operations to be used to easily and fully recover this symbolic structure, including its compositional structure.

Constructing a TPR for a linguistic unit (such as a morpheme or a word) begins by decomposing the symbolic structure of that unit into *roles* and *fillers*. Each role represents a linguistic feature, while each filler represents the actual value of that feature.

The symbolic structure of a word is then represented as the *bindings* of fillers to roles for all feature-value pairs associated with that unit. Once decomposed, both roles and fillers are embedded into a vector space such that all roles are linearly independent from one another. Let b be a list of ordered pairs (i, j) representing filler i (with embedding vector $\hat{\mathbf{f}}_i$) being bound to role j (with embedding vector $\hat{\mathbf{r}}_j$). The *tensor product representation* $\mathbf{T}$ of the information is then given by

$$\mathbf{T} = \sum_{(i,j)\in b} \hat{\mathbf{f}}_i \otimes \hat{\mathbf{r}}_j \in \mathbb{R}^d \otimes \mathbb{R}^n. \quad (1)$$

3.3 Constructing a TPR from an ILG

Our use of TPRs to represent ILGs is meant to be agnostic to linguistic theory. Considerable flexibility is available to the computational linguist in determining exactly how to map linguistic features from an ILG into the structure of a TPR. For example, one TPR design choice might involve linguistic features such as noun case or verb mood serving as roles, while the corresponding fillers represent actual values of those features, such as associative case or indicative mood.

For the sake of expositional simplicity in presenting a multilingual and typologically diverse set of linguistic examples (and without loss of generality), in Examples (1) and (2) below and in §4 we opt for a simplistic linguistic mapping where each TPR role represents a (grapheme or morpheme) position within the word and where the corresponding TPR fillers represent (grapheme or morpheme) identity at that position. Concretely, given a word comprised of ℓ graphemes and m morphemes, $\hat{\mathbf{r}}_i$ and $\hat{\mathbf{r}}_{m_j}$ are one-hot[6] vectors respectively representing grapheme position i (where $0 \leq i < \ell$) and morpheme position j (where $0 \leq j < m$) within the word. For each linguistic element (grapheme or morpheme) γ in the language, $\hat{\mathbf{f}}_\gamma$ is a vector[7] representing that element.

We now illustrate how morpheme and word embeddings can be constructed from interlinear glosses, using the English words 'dog' and 'dogs as Examples (1) and (2), respectively.

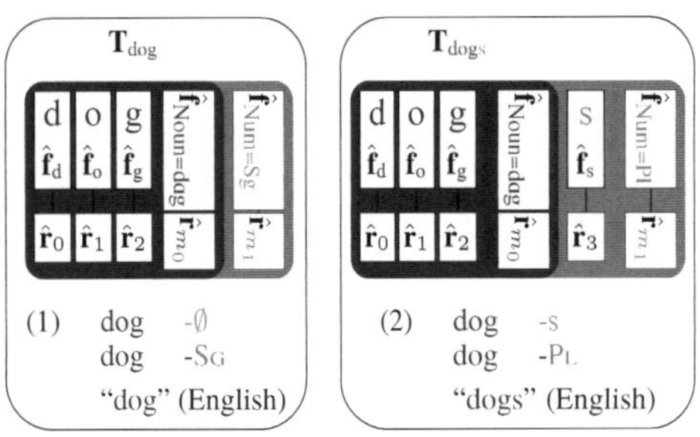

Each example is shown within a rounded rectangle; the example number and interlinear gloss are found at the bottom of the rounded rectangle, while a visualization of the TPR is shown at the top of the rectangle. At the top of each example is a label for the resulting word embedding. Colors are used to differentiate morpheme positions within the word.

In Example (1), $\hat{\mathbf{r}}_0$ is a one-hot vector representing the initial grapheme position within the word, and $\hat{\mathbf{f}}_{\text{d}}$ is a one-hot vector representing the English letter 'd'. The outer product $\hat{\mathbf{r}}_0 \otimes \hat{\mathbf{f}}_{\text{d}}$ now represents a one-hot matrix encoding that the grapheme at position 0 is the English letter 'd'. Applying Equation (1), we add together three one-hot matrices ($\hat{\mathbf{r}}_0 \otimes \hat{\mathbf{f}}_{\text{d}} + \hat{\mathbf{r}}_1 \otimes \hat{\mathbf{f}}_{\text{o}} + \hat{\mathbf{r}}_2 \otimes \hat{\mathbf{f}}_{\text{g}}$), to obtain a sparse matrix that encodes the surface form of the morpheme 'dog.' Similarly, $\hat{\mathbf{r}}_{m_0} \otimes \hat{\mathbf{f}}_{\text{Noun=dog}}$ encodes that the identity of the initial morpheme in Example (1) is the noun 'dog.'

Recursive applications of Equation (1) result in multi-dimensional tensors $\mathbf{T}_{\text{dog}}$ (encoding the surface form and morpheme identity of each morpheme in the word 'dog') and $\mathbf{T}_{\text{dogs}}$ (encoding the surface form and morpheme identity of each morpheme in the word "dogs').

3.4 Dense vectors from TPRs

Depending on how much linguistic information is encoded, each TPRs may consist of approximately 10^3 to 10^9 floating point values per tensor. Tensors of this size are far too large to be directly usable as neural word representations. It is therefore necessary to map each sparse TPR into an equivalent dense vector representation. Any of several existing techniques may be used to achieve this task; for simplicity in our work to date, we make use of an autoencoder. The autoencoder is trained using a dictionary of word or morpheme TPRs. The trained autoencoder can be used to encode a low-dimensional vector from a high-dimensional tensor by running the tensor through the first half of the autoencoder, and can be used to reconstitute the high-dimensional tensor from a vector by running the vector though the latter half of the autoencoder. For additional details, see Appendix A.

4 Supporting full linguistic diversity

We now demonstrate the broad applicability of our technique for encoding rich linguistic information from morphologically analyses such as ILGs using examples drawn from a typologically diverse set of polysynthetic, agglutinative, fusional, and analytic languages. The following examples include prefixes, suffixes, infixes, circumfixes, templatic morphemes, derivational morphemes, inflectional morphemes, and reduplication. The notation in the

[6]In the general case, role vectors need not necessarily be one-hot.

[7]For simplicity in our case, these filler vectors are one-hot. In the general case, filler vectors need not necessarily be one-hot, and may be separately pre-trained grapheme or morpheme embeddings if desired.

following examples follows the conventions established in §3.3.

4.1 Concatenative morphology and zero inflection in English

Concatenative morphology is extremely common cross-linguistically. Examples (1) and (2) in §3.3 demonstrate basic concatenative morphology in the English words 'dog' and 'dogs'. Example (1) illustrates that linguistic features of a word can be encoded even when those features are not explicitly marked in the surface form of the word. In Example (1), the tensor $\mathbf{T}_{\text{dog}}$ explicitly encodes the null singular morpheme -∅ marking number as singular in the word 'dog,' just as the morpheme -s marks number as plural in the word 'dogs in Example (2).' Unlike existing representations discussed in §2, $\mathbf{T}_{\text{dog}}$ and $\mathbf{T}_{\text{dogs}}$ are clearly distinguishable as variant inflections of the same root word.

4.2 Circumfixes in Chukchi

The Chukchi[8] word гаԓявтыма is composed of a noun root morpheme ɬawət and an inflectional circumfix ɣa…ma. The tensor $\mathbf{T}_{\text{гаԓявтыма}}$ is a TPR that represents this word, ***explicitly including*** all information shown in Example (3):

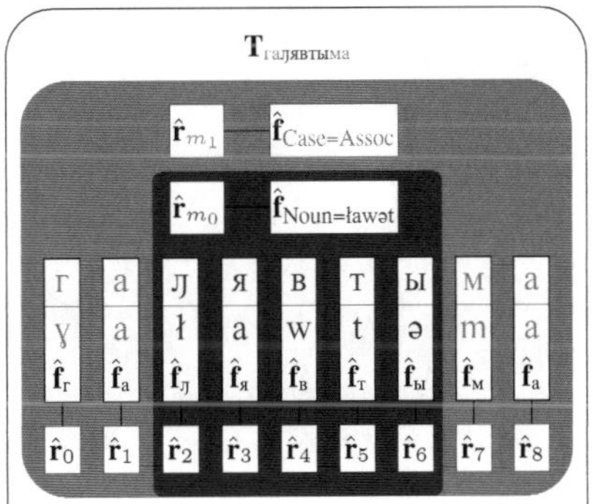

(3) ɣa- ɬewət -ma
Assoc- head -Assoc
"with the head" (Chukchi)

The individual characters positions in the word comprise roles $\hat{\mathbf{r}}_0$ through $\hat{\mathbf{r}}_8$, while the characters (and respective phonemes) at those respective positions comprise fillers $\hat{\mathbf{f}}_{\text{г}}$, $\hat{\mathbf{f}}_{\text{а}}$, $\hat{\mathbf{f}}_{\text{ԓ}}$, $\hat{\mathbf{f}}_{\text{я}}$, $\hat{\mathbf{f}}_{\text{в}}$, $\hat{\mathbf{f}}_{\text{т}}$, $\hat{\mathbf{f}}_{\text{ы}}$, and $\hat{\mathbf{f}}_{\text{м}}$ that encode character and phoneme identity. Roles $\hat{\mathbf{r}}_{m_0}$ and $\hat{\mathbf{r}}_{m_1}$ represent morpheme positions within the word, and are respectively filled by $\hat{\mathbf{f}}_{\text{Noun=ɬawət}}$ (denoting the identity of the root morpheme) and $\hat{\mathbf{f}}_{\text{Case=Assoc}}$ (denoting the identity of the circumfix morpheme marking associative case).

4.3 Fusional suffixes in Catalan

Fusional morphology is also common cross-linguistics, as we can see in the Catalan[9] word tinc in Example (4), which is comprised only of only a verb root ten- 'to have' and a single inflectional suffix marking person, number, tense, and mood.

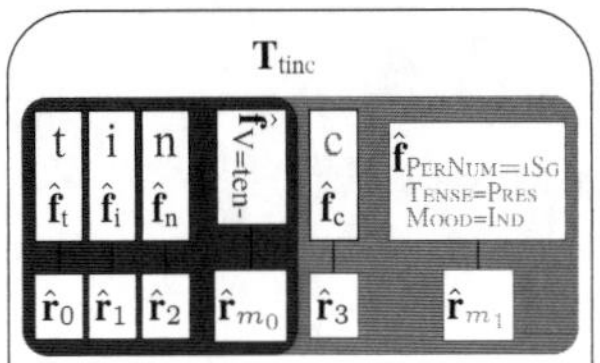

(4) tinc
ten -c
to.have -1Sg.Pres.Ind
"I have" (Catalan)

4.4 Polysynthesis with derivational and inflectional suffixes in Akuzipik

Productive derivational and inflectional suffixes are pervasive in the polysynthetic languages of the Inuit-Yupik language family. Words with 2-5 derivational morphemes are very common, often representing in a single word what in English would be represented by an entire clause or sentence.

The Akuzipik[10] word mangteghaghrugllangllaghyunghitunga shown in Example (5) can be translated into English as the sentence 'I didn't want to make a huge house' (Jacobson, 2001, pg. 43). The tensor $\mathbf{T}_{\text{mangteghaghrugllangllaghyunghitunga}}$ encodes the hierarchical structure of this word. Each grapheme position within the word is assigned a role ($\hat{\mathbf{r}}_0 \ldots \hat{\mathbf{r}}_{25}$). For each of these grapheme position roles, a filler vector encodes the identity of the grapheme and corresponding phoneme at that position in the word ($\hat{\mathbf{f}}_0 \ldots \hat{\mathbf{f}}_{25}$). The binding of grapheme position roles to grapheme filler vectors represents the first level of hierarchy in the TPR. The word is composed of 7 morphemes: a noun root maŋtəʁaʁ, four derivational morphemes (-ʁɹuxɬaɣ, -ŋ̊ɬaʁ, -juɣ, -nʁitə) and two inflectional morphemes (-tu and -ŋa). The subsequent levels of the TPR encode the identity, underlying form, surface form, and hierarchical scope of each

[8]ISO 639-3: *ckt*, a polysynthetic language in the Chukotkan branch of the Chukotko–Kamchatkan language family

[9]ISO 639-3: *cat*, a fusional language in the Romance branch of the Indo-European language family

[10]ISO 639-3: *ess*, a polysynthetic language in the Yupik branch of the Inuit-Yupik-Unangan language family

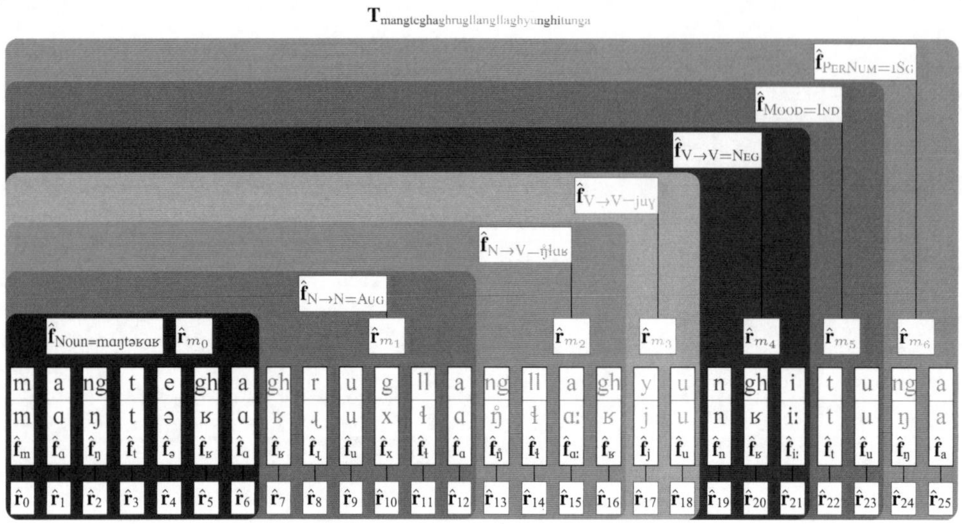

(5)	maŋtəʁaʁ	-ʁɻuxɬaɣ	-ŋ̊ɬaʁ	-juɣ	-nʁitə	-tu	-ŋa
	house	AUG	build	want	NEG	IND	1SG

'I didn't want to make a huge house' (Akuzipik)

morpheme. The resulting word representation is compositional and easily interpretable.

By inspecting the resulting tensor, the following structure of the word can be clearly observed:

- The noun root for 'house' maŋtəʁaʁ is modified by the augmentatitive derivational morpheme -ʁɻuxɬaɣ, resulting in an extended noun stem meaning 'big house' spanning grapheme positions 0 through 12.
- The resulting extended noun stem (maŋtəʁaʁɻuxɬaɣ) is verbalized by the derivational morpheme -ŋ̊ɬaʁ, resulting in an extended verb stem meaning 'to build a big house' spanning grapheme positions 0 through 16.
- The resulting extended verb stem (maŋtəʁaʁɻuxɬaŋ̊ɬaʁ) is modified by the derivational morpheme -juɣ, resulting in an extended verb stem meaning 'to want to build a big house' spanning grapheme positions 0 through 18.
- The resulting extended verb stem (maŋtəʁaʁɻuxɬaŋ̊ɬaʁjuɣ) is modified by the negating derivational morpheme -nʁitə), resulting in an extended verb stem meaning 'to not want to build a big house' spanning grapheme positions 0 through 21.
- The resulting extended verb stem (maŋtəʁaʁɻuxɬaŋ̊ɬaʁjunʁitə) is marked as being in the indicative mood by the inflectional morpheme -tu and as having a first person singular subject by the inflectional morpheme -ŋa, resulting in the fully inflected word spanning grapheme positions 0 through 25.

4.5 Agglutination in Guaraní

In the Guaraní[11] word aikosente shown in Example (6), the verb root ko 'to live' is modified in agglutinative manner by two suffixes (-se and -nte) and one inflectional prefix (ai-) which indicates a first person singular subject. Note that unlike the preceding example, which also encoded phoneme identity, in this example character fillers encode only character identity.

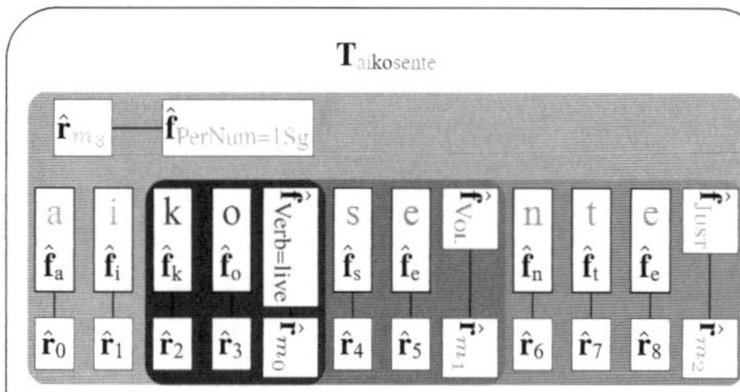

(6) aikosente

ai-	ko	-se	-nte
SG1-	live	-VOL	-JUST

'I would just like to live' (Guaraní)

[11]ISO 639-3: *gug*, an agglutinative language in the Tupian language family

4.6 Infixation in English

Linguistic features such as infixes that are attested but relatively rare can also be included with no difficulty. Infixes are morphemes that break a given stem and appear inside it. In Seri,[12] for example, infixation after the first vowel in the root is used to mark number agreement. In Example (7), we observe an example of expletive infixation in English (McCarthy, 1982) with the infix fuckin serving to intensify the adverb absolutely.

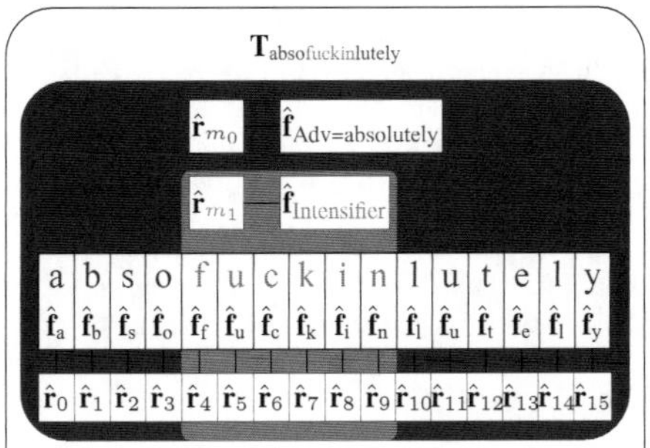

(7) abso- fuckin -lutely
abso- INTENSIFIER -lutely
"absofuckinlutely" (English)

4.7 Reduplication in Malaysian

The Malaysian[13] word orang-orang 'people', is formed through reduplication of the noun root orang 'person'. Unlike in previous examples, in which morpheme fillers encoded underlying lexical form in addition to morpheme surface form and identity, in Example (8), the plural morpheme has no inherent underlying lexical form separate from the morpheme identity (NUM=PL). Instead the surface form of the plural morpheme (here, orang) is formed through reduplication, duplicating the form of the noun to which it attaches.

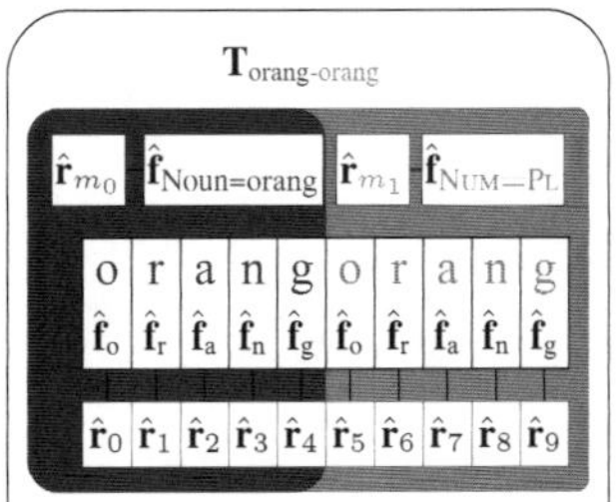

(8) orang -orang
orang -PL
"people" (Malaysian)

4.8 Templatic morphology in Maltese

Our representation can easily encode non-concatenative morphology such as that seen in the Maltese[14] words ktieb 'book' and kotba 'books.'

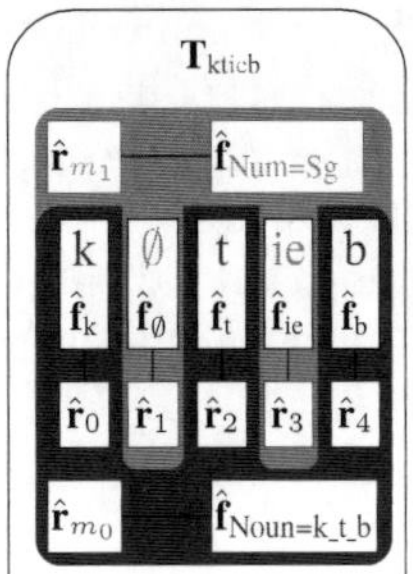

(9) ktieb
k_t_b ∅_ie
book SG
"book" (Maltese)

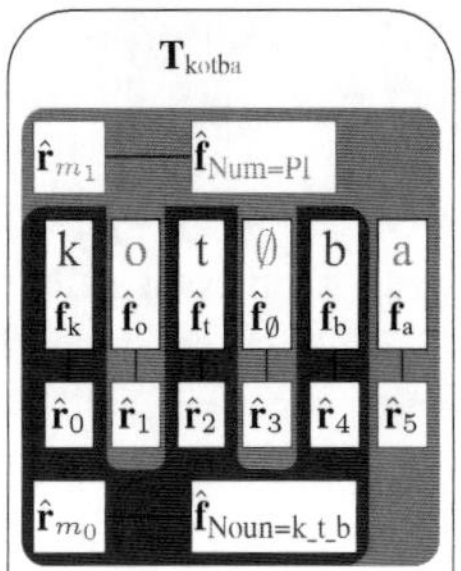

(10) kotba
k_t_b o_∅_a
book PL
"books" (Maltese)

The noun root k_t_b acts as a template whose slots are filled by the vowels in the inflectional singular morpheme ∅_ie (in Example (9)) or plural morpheme o_∅_a (in Example (10)).

5 Conclusion

While corpora of anything greater than trivial size exist only for a few hundred languages (§1), morphologically analyzed examples in the form of interlinear glosses exist for essentially every human language. The vast array of human languages include a rich variety of morphological phenomenon that are not easily handled by existing word embedding methods (§2). This work presents a straightforward mechanism whereby meaningful, linguistically interpretable word and morpheme embeddings can be created for any word in any language (§3–§4). We have demonstrated the applicability of our method using linguistic examples of concatenation and zero inflection (§4.1), circumfixation (§4.2), fusion (§4.3), polysynthesis (§4.4), agglutination (§4.5), infixation (§4.6), reduplication (§4.7), and templatic morphology (§4.8).

In addition to their direct use in future research involving language documentation and revitalization, we anticipate that embeddings created using the methods described in this work may provide an important initial step in bootstrapping vastly multilingual models capable of embedding words from thousands of languages.

[12] ISO 639-3: *sei* a language isolate in north-west Mexico

[13] ISO 639-3: *zsm*, a language in the Malayo-Polynesian branch of the Austronesian language family

[14] ISO 639-3: *mlt*, a templatic language in the Semitic language family

Acknowledgements

This work was initially developed during the 2019 JSALT workshop on Neural Polysynthetic Language Modelling (Schwartz et al., 2020b) in Montréal, Canada. We wish to express our appreciation to the organizers, sponsors, and hosts of the 2019 JSALT workshop. We wish to express our deep respect and thanks to the many peoples whose languages we present in the examples in this paper. We wish to acknowledge and honor the Indigenous peoples on whose lands we live and work, both at Montréal and at our individual universities.

Our code is at `https://github.com/neural-polysynthetic-language-modelling/iiksiin` and the scripts we used to run our code are at `https://github.com/neural-polysynthetic-language-modelling/iiksiin.experiment`

References

Jesujoba Alabi, Kwabena Amponsah-Kaakyire, David Adelani, and Cristina España-Bonet. 2020. Massive vs. curated embeddings for low-resourced languages: the case of Yorùbá and Twi. In *Proceedings of the 12th Language Resources and Evaluation Conference*, pages 2754–2762, Marseille, France. European Language Resources Association.

Kenneth R. Beesley and Lauri Karttunen. 2003. *Finite State Morphology*. CSLI Studies in Computational Linguistics. CSLI Publications, Stanford, California.

Emily M. Bender. 2011. On achieving and evaluating language-independence in NLP. *Linguistic Issues in Language Technology*, 6(3):1–26.

Balthasar Bickel and Johanna Nichols. 2013. Inflectional synthesis of the verb. In Matthew S. Dryer and Martin Haspelmath, editors, *The World Atlas of Language Structures Online*. Max Planck Institute for Evolutionary Anthropology, Leipzig.

Peter F. Brown, Stephen A. Della Pietra, Vincent J. Della Pietra, and Robert L. Mercer. 1993. The mathematics of statistical machine translation: Parameter estimation. *Computational Linguistics*, 19(2):263–311.

Emrah Budur, Rıza Özçelik, Tunga Gungor, and Christopher Potts. 2020. Data and Representation for Turkish Natural Language Inference. In *Proceedings of the 2020 Conference on Empirical Methods in Natural Language Processing (EMNLP)*, pages 8253–8267, Online. Association for Computational Linguistics.

William E. Bull, Charles Africa, and Daniel Teichroew. 1955. Some problems of the "word". In William N. Locke and A. Donald Booth, editors, *Machine Translations of Languages*. Greenwood Press, Westport, Connecticut.

Emily Chen and Lane Schwartz. 2018. A morphological analyzer for St. Lawrence Island / Central Siberian Yupik. In *Proceedings of the 11th Language Resources and Evaluation Conference (LREC 2018)*, Miyazaki, Japan. European Languages Resources Association (ELRA).

Kenneth Church. 2011. A pendulum swung too far. *Linguistic Issues in Language Technology*, 6(3):1–27.

Kenneth W. Church and Robert L. Mercer. 1993. Introduction to the special issue on computational linguistics using large corpora. *Computational Linguistics*, 19(1):1–24.

Jonathan H. Clark, Dan Garrette, Iulia Turc, and John Wieting. 2022. Canine: Pre-training an efficient tokenization-free encoder for language representation. *Transactions of the Association for Computational Linguistics*, 10:73–91.

Alexis Conneau, Kartikay Khandelwal, Naman Goyal, Vishrav Chaudhary, Guillaume Wenzek, Francisco Guzmán, Edouard Grave, Myle Ott, Luke Zettlemoyer, and Veselin Stoyanov. 2020. Unsupervised cross-lingual representation learning at scale. In *Proceedings of the 58th Annual Meeting of the Association for Computational Linguistics*, pages 8440–8451, Online. Association for Computational Linguistics.

Mathias Creutz and Krista Lagus. 2002. Unsupervised discovery of morphemes. In *Proceedings of the ACL-02 Workshop on Morphological and Phonological Learning*, pages 21–30. Association for Computational Linguistics.

Jacob Devlin, Ming-Wei Chang, Kenton Lee, and Kristina Toutanova. 2019. BERT: Pre-training of deep bidirectional transformers for language understanding. In *Proceedings of the 2019 Conference of the North American Chapter of the Association for Computational Linguistics: Human Language Technologies, Volume 1 (Long and Short Papers)*, pages 4171–4186, Minneapolis, Minnesota. Association for Computational Linguistics.

Matthew S. Dryer. 2013. Prefixing vs. suffixing in inflectional morphology. In Matthew S. Dryer and Martin Haspelmath, editors, *The World Atlas of Language Structures Online*. Max Planck Institute for Evolutionary Anthropology, Leipzig.

Matthew S. Dryer and Martin Haspelmath, editors. 2013. *World Atlas of Language Structures*. Max Planck Institute for Evolutionary Anthropology, Leipzig.

Tobias Eder, Viktor Hangya, and Alexander Fraser. 2021. Anchor-based bilingual word embeddings for low-resource languages. In *Proceedings of the*

59th Annual Meeting of the Association for Computational Linguistics and the 11th International Joint Conference on Natural Language Processing (Volume 2: Short Papers), pages 227–232, Online. Association for Computational Linguistics.

Coleman Haley and Paul Smolensky. 2020. Invertible tree embeddings using a cryptographic role embedding scheme. In *Proceedings of the 28th International Conference on Computational Linguistics*, pages 3671–3683, Barcelona, Spain (Online). International Committee on Computational Linguistics.

Michael A. Hedderich, Lukas Lange, Heike Adel, Jannik Strötgen, and Dietrich Klakow. 2021. A survey on recent approaches for natural language processing in low-resource scenarios. In *Proceedings of the 2021 Conference of the North American Chapter of the Association for Computational Linguistics: Human Language Technologies*, pages 2545–2568, Online. Association for Computational Linguistics.

G.E. Hinton, J.L. McClelland, and D.E. Rumelhart. 1986. Distributed representations. In *Parallel distributed processing: Explorations in the microstructure of cognition*, volume 1: Foundations. MIT Press.

W. John Hutchins. 1986. *Machine Translation: Past, Present, Future*. Computers and Their Applications. Ellis Horwood.

Steven A. Jacobson. 2001. *A Practical Grammar of the St. Lawrence Island / Siberian Yupik Eskimo Language, Preliminary Edition*, 2nd edition. Alaska Native Language Center, Fairbanks, Alaska.

Pratik Joshi, Sebastin Santy, Amar Budhiraja, Kalika Bali, and Monojit Choudhury. 2020. The state and fate of linguistic diversity and inclusion in the NLP world. In *Proceedings of the 58th Annual Meeting of the Association for Computational Linguistics*, pages 6282–6293, Online. Association for Computational Linguistics.

Philipp Koehn. 2010. *Statistical Machine Translation*. Cambridge University Press, Cambridge, UK.

Taku Kudo and John Richardson. 2018. SentencePiece: A simple and language independent subword tokenizer and detokenizer for neural text processing. In *Proceedings of the 2018 Conference on Empirical Methods in Natural Language Processing: System Demonstrations*, pages 66–71, Brussels, Belgium. Association for Computational Linguistics.

Christopher D. Manning and Hinrich Schütze. 1999. *Foundations of Statistical Natural Language Processing*. MIT Press, Cambridge, Massachusetts.

John J. McCarthy. 1982. Prosodic structure and expletive infixation. *Language*, 58(3):574–590.

Leah Michel, Viktor Hangya, and Alexander Fraser. 2020. Exploring bilingual word embeddings for Hiligaynon, a low-resource language. In *Proceedings of the 12th Language Resources and Evaluation Conference*, pages 2573–2580, Marseille, France. European Language Resources Association.

Tomás Mikolov, Kai Chen, Greg Corrado, and Jeffrey Dean. 2013a. Efficient estimation of word representations in vector space. In *1st International Conference on Learning Representations, ICLR 2013, Scottsdale, Arizona, USA, May 2-4, 2013, Workshop Track Proceedings*.

Tomas Mikolov, Wen-tau Yih, and Geoffrey Zweig. 2013b. Linguistic regularities in continuous space word representations. In *Proceedings of the 2013 Conference of the North American Chapter of the Association for Computational Linguistics: Human Language Technologies*, pages 746–751, Atlanta, Georgia. Association for Computational Linguistics.

Anthony Oettinger. 1954. *A Study for the Design of an Automatic Dictionary*. Ph.D. thesis, Harvard University, Cambridge, Massachusetts.

Hyunji Hayley Park, Katherine J. Zhang, Coleman Haley, Kenneth Steimel, Han Liu, and Lane Schwartz. 2021. Morphology Matters: A Multilingual Language Modeling Analysis. *Transactions of the Association for Computational Linguistics*, 9:261–276.

Jeffrey Pennington, Richard Socher, and Christopher Manning. 2014. GloVe: Global vectors for word representation. In *Proceedings of the 2014 Conference on Empirical Methods in Natural Language Processing (EMNLP)*, pages 1532–1543, Doha, Qatar. Association for Computational Linguistics.

Matthew E. Peters, Mark Neumann, Mohit Iyyer, Matt Gardner, Christopher Clark, Kenton Lee, and Luke Zettlemoyer. 2018. Deep contextualized word representations. In *Proceedings of the 2018 Conference of the North American Chapter of the Association for Computational Linguistics: Human Language Technologies, Volume 1 (Long Papers)*, pages 2227–2237, New Orleans, Louisiana. Association for Computational Linguistics.

Carl Pollard and Ivan A. Sag. 1994. *Head-Driven Phrase Structure Grammar*. University of Chicago Press.

Edoardo Maria Ponti, Helen O'Horan, Yevgeni Berzak, Ivan Vulić, Roi Reichart, Thierry Poibeau, Ekaterina Shutova, and Anna Korhonen. 2019. Modeling language variation and universals: A survey on typological linguistics for natural language processing. *Computational Linguistics*, 45(3):559–601.

Anna Rogers, Olga Kovaleva, and Anna Rumshisky. 2020. A primer in BERTology: What we know about how BERT works. *Transactions of the Association for Computational Linguistics*, 8:842–866.

Lane Schwartz, Sylvia Schreiner, and Emily Chen. 2020a. Community-focused language documentation in support of language education and revitalization for St. Lawrence Island Yupik. *Études Inuit Studies*, 43(1–2):291–312.

Lane Schwartz, Francis Tyers, Lori Levin, Christo Kirov, Patrick Littell, Chi-kiu Lo, Emily Prud'hommeaux, Hyunji Hayley Park, Kenneth Steimel, Rebecca Knowles, Jeffrey Micher, Lonny Strunk, Han Liu, Coleman Haley, Katherine J. Zhang, Robbie Jimmerson, Vasilisa Andriyanets, Aldrian Obaja Muis, Naoki Otani, Jong Hyuk Park, and Zhisong Zhang. 2020b. Neural polysynthetic language modelling. Final Report of the Neural Polysynthetic Language Modelling Team at the 2019 Frederick Jelinek Memorial Summer Workshop.

Rico Sennrich, Barry Haddow, and Alexandra Birch. 2016. Neural machine translation of rare words with subword units. In *Proceedings of the 54th Annual Meeting of the Association for Computational Linguistics (Volume 1: Long Papers)*, pages 1715–1725, Berlin, Germany. Association for Computational Linguistics.

Peter Smit, Sami Virpioja, Stig-Arne Grönroos, and Mikko Kurimo. 2014. Morfessor 2.0: Toolkit for statistical morphological segmentation. In *Proceedings of the Demonstrations at the 14th Conference of the European Chapter of the Association for Computational Linguistics*, pages 21–24, Gothenburg, Sweden. Association for Computational Linguistics.

Paul Smolensky. 1990. Tensor product variable binding and the representation of symbolic structures in connectionist systems. *Artificial Intelligence*, 46:159–216.

Laurent Vannini and Hervé Le Crosnier, editors. 2012. *Net.lang: Towards the Multilingual Cyberspace*. C&F éditions.

Ashish Vaswani, Noam Shazeer, Niki Parmar, Jakob Uszkoreit, Llion Jones, Aidan N Gomez, Ł ukasz Kaiser, and Illia Polosukhin. 2017. Attention is all you need. In *Advances in Neural Information Processing Systems*, volume 30. Curran Associates, Inc.

Shijie Wu and Mark Dredze. 2020. Are all languages created equal in multilingual BERT? In *Proceedings of the 5th Workshop on Representation Learning for NLP*, pages 120–130, Online. Association for Computational Linguistics.

Yonghui Wu, Mike Schuster, Zhifeng Chen, Quoc V. Le, Mohammad Norouzi, Wolfgang Macherey, Maxim Krikun, Yuan Cao, Qin Gao, Klaus Macherey, Jeff Klingner, Apurva Shah, Melvin Johnson, Xiaobing Liu, Lukasz Kaiser, Stephan Gouws, Yoshikiyo Kato, Taku Kudo, Hideto Kazawa, Keith Stevens, George Kurian, Nishant Patil, Wei Wang, Cliff Young, Jason Smith, Jason Riesa, Alex Rudnick, Oriol Vinyals, Greg Corrado, Macduff Hughes, and Jeffrey Dean. 2016. Google's neural machine translation system: Bridging the gap between human and machine translation. *CoRR*, abs/1609.08144.

Zhengyan Zhang, Xu Han, Zhiyuan Liu, Xin Jiang, Maosong Sun, and Qun Liu. 2019. ERNIE: Enhanced language representation with informative entities. In *Proceedings of the 57th Annual Meeting of the Association for Computational Linguistics*, pages 1441–1451, Florence, Italy. Association for Computational Linguistics.

Junru Zhou, Zuchao Li, and Hai Zhao. 2020a. Parsing all: Syntax and semantics, dependencies and spans. In *Findings of the Association for Computational Linguistics: EMNLP 2020*, pages 4438–4449, Online. Association for Computational Linguistics.

Junru Zhou, Zhuosheng Zhang, Hai Zhao, and Shuailiang Zhang. 2020b. LIMIT-BERT : Linguistics informed multi-task BERT. In *Findings of the Association for Computational Linguistics: EMNLP 2020*, pages 4450–4461, Online. Association for Computational Linguistics.

A Unbinding

The core operation in retrieving structure from a TPR is called *unbinding*. Exact unbinding requires linear independence of the roles; however, Haley and Smolensky (2020) present an accurate approximate unbinding strategy for even densely packed TPRs. In this work, we use self-addressing unbinding, as it is quick to compute and proved sufficiently accurate for our purposes. Self-addressing unbinding retrieves the filler $\tilde{\mathbf{f}}_i$ for the role $\hat{\mathbf{r}}_i$ by simply computing the inner product between the role vector and the TPR:

$$\tilde{\mathbf{f}}_i = \mathbf{T} \cdot \hat{\mathbf{r}}_i \tag{2}$$

This unbinding is exact if the role vectors are orthogonal to one another. In our case, since we have a fixed filler vocabulary, we were able to snap our unbindings to the filler with the highest cosine similarity to the unbound vector with sufficient accuracy to render this intrusion irrelevant. Other unbinding strategies involve computing an inverse or pseudoinverse of a matrix of role vectors to perform a change of basis and decrease the intrusion.

A.1 Unbinding loss

In order to effectively train the autoencoder in §3.4, gold standard TPRs must be compared against predicted tensors reconstituted by the autoencoder. However, these tensors are very high dimensional. In initial experiments, we used mean squared error as a loss function, but we found this was unable to converge for auto-encoding sparse TPRs.

To enable effective training of the autoencoder, we therefore define a novel loss function that makes use of the information encoded in the TPR. We define a loss function called *unbinding loss* that examines the unbinding properties of a predicted morpheme tensor to answer the question, "What filler is closest to the unbinding of each role in the TPR?"

Given a predicted tensor, the unbinding loss is computed by recursively unbinding roles until the leaves of the structure are reached – that is, unbind each role until the result of unbinding is a single vector (rather than a higher-order tensor). When this point is reached, we compute the cosine similarity between the result of unbinding and all the fillers in the vocabulary.

This similarity vector can be used to define a probability distribution over possible fillers through the use of a softmax. We take the logarithm of the result of this computation to obtain log-probabilities. We call this distribution P. We then treat each filler (in this case, each character) as a class, and compute the negative log-likelihood loss over this probability distribution.

As we consider tree-structured representations, the number of fillers needing to be checked is exponential with the depth of our representation. This difficulty could be overcome by parallelizing the independent matrix computations for the loss of all the position roles for a given morpheme, trading space for time. For more complex TPRs, a potential avenue would be to exploit the fact that most roles will be empty (and their unbindings thus a matrix of zeros) by replacing the loss computations for unbound roles with mean squared error (which need only push that part of the representation to 0).

A.2 Unbinding loss example

Given a predicted tensor, the first step to computing the unbinding loss is recursively unbinding roles until the leaves of the structure are reached – that is, unbind each role until the result of unbinding is a single vector (rather than a higher-order tensor). When this point is reached, we compute the cosine similarity between the result of unbinding and all the fillers in the vocabulary. For example, assume a depth-4 structure is encoded in a morpheme TPR $\mathbf{T}$, where the fillers are character embeddings, the second level is left-to-right positional roles, the third level is morpheme identity, and the fourth level is left-to-right morpheme position in the word. If we want to see what is bound to the first position of the English *dog* morpheme in $\mathbf{T}$, we would first unbind from $\mathbf{T}$ as follows (assuming self-addressing unbinding):

$$\mathbf{f}_{dog,1} = \mathbf{T} \cdot \hat{\mathbf{r}}_{m0} \cdot \hat{\mathbf{f}}_{Noun=dog} \cdot \hat{\mathbf{r}}_1 \quad (3)$$

We then get the vector of similarities $\hat{\mathbf{s}}_{dog,1}$ between this filler and the each of character embedding vectors in the vocabulary matrix V as follows:

$$\hat{\mathbf{s}}_{dog,1} = \frac{\mathbf{f}_{dog,1} \cdot \mathbf{V}}{||\mathbf{f}_{dog,1}||\mathbf{V}^i\mathbf{V}^i} \quad (4)$$

where $\mathbf{V}^i\mathbf{V}^i$ denotes the column-wise vector norm of the vocabulary matrix (using Einstein summation notation).

This similarity vector can be used to define a probability distribution over possible fillers through the use of a softmax. We take the logarithm of the result of this computation to obtain log-probabilities. We call this distribution P.

$$P = \log\left(\frac{e^{\hat{\mathbf{s}}_{dog,1}}}{\sum e^{\hat{\mathbf{s}}_{dog,1}}}\right) \quad (5)$$

We then treat each filler (in this case, each character) as a class, and compute the negative log-likelihood loss over this probability distribution. The resulting loss for the first character of *dog* being "d" is then

$$loss(\hat{\mathbf{s}}_{dog,1}, d) = -\hat{\mathbf{s}}_{dog,1,d} + \log(\sum_j e^{\hat{\mathbf{s}}_{dog,1,j}}). \quad (6)$$

If the Tensor this loss is computed over is exactly $\mathbf{T}_{\text{dog}}$ or $\mathbf{T}_{\text{dogs}}$, then this loss term would be 0. If we instead considered the loss for the fourth character of the word being "s" in the Num=Pl morpheme, This would be 0 only for $\mathbf{T}_{\text{dogs}}$.

A.3 Successfully recovering surface forms from vectors

To demonstrate the successful recovery of linguistic data from embeddings, we construct TPRs for a dictionary of 6372 unique Akuzipik morpheme surface forms obtained by applying the finite-state morphological analyzer of Chen and Schwartz (2018) on a selection of Akuzupik New Testament data from `https://github.com/SaintLawrenceIslandYupik/digital_corpus`. Using TPRs constructed from these morphemes, we trained a 3-layer autoencoder with vector sizes of 64, 128, 256, and 512 using unbinding loss (§A.1) as the loss function. We then reconstructed the morpheme surface forms from the trained morpheme vectors. For vector size of 64, the reconstructed morpheme surface form exactly matched the original morpheme surface form for 97.8% of the morphemes. For vector sizes of 128, 256, and 512, the morpheme surface form reconstruction accuracy was 100%.

Predictive Text for Agglutinative and Polysynthetic Languages

Sergey Kosyak
School of Linguistics,
Higher School of Economics
Moscow, Russian Federation
skosiak@hse.ru

Francis M. Tyers
Department of Linguistics,
Indiana University
IN, United States of America
ftyers@iu.edu

Abstract

This paper presents a set of experiments in the area of morphological modelling and prediction. We test whether morphological segmentation can compete against statistical segmentation in the tasks of language modelling and predictive text entry for two under-resourced and indigenous languages, K'iche' and Chukchi. We use different segmentation methods – both statistical and morphological – to make datasets that are used to train models of different types: single-way segmented, which are trained using data from one segmenter; two-way segmented, which are trained using concatenated data from two segmenters; and finetuned, which are trained on two datasets from different segmenters. We compute word and character level perplexities and find that single-way segmented models trained on morphologically segmented data show the highest performance. Finally, we evaluate the language models on the task of predictive text entry using gold standard data and measure the average number of clicks per character and keystroke savings rate. We find that the models trained on morphologically segmented data show better scores, although with substantial room for improvement. At last, we propose the usage of morphological segmentation in order to improve the end-user experience while using predictive text and we plan on testing this assumption by doing end-user evaluation.

1 Introduction

Nowadays text prediction is widely used in different applications such as autocomplete tools, smart keyboards, etc. The used language models are limited by resources, so they can store only the top-N highest frequency words, which may work well with analytic languages, but when it comes to the synthetic languages the out-of-vocabulary (OOV) problem becomes more and more noticeable. In order to deal with this problem, words are usually segmented in constituent parts, so that more of them can be saved in the model vocabulary. Segmentation is almost always done using statistical methods, such as BPE (Gage, 1994). In this paper, we test whether morphological segmentation can improve language modelling and whether it can compete against statistical segmentation methods in predictive text entry task.

The reason to suggest morphological segmentation is that we want text prediction to be both effective and *ergonomic*. By ergonomic we mean that predictions should be linguistically sound and intelligible for the end user. For example, imagine an English word *antidisestablishmentarianism*. An ergonomic segmentation will split the word into its constituent morphs [anti, dis, establish, ment, arian, ism], or an alternative [anti, dis, establishment, arianism]. An unergonomic segmentation might be [antid, isestab, lishme, ntarianism] or [an, tidises, tablishm, entarianism]. One of the issues with many current methods is that while they can produce segments that are meaningful units, in many cases the segments are not linguistically meaningful. We argue that for the task of predictive text entry producing non-linguistic units creates more cognitive load and so will result in slower text entry than predicting the same amount (or a greater number of) linguistic units.

The remainder of the paper is laid out as follows: in Section 2 we overview the languages we experiment on, in Section 3 we discuss the works that were an inspiration for this paper, in Section 4 we describe the experiments we are doing, in Section 5 we review the used segmentation methods, in Section 6 we provide results of language modelling, in Section 7 we speak about language modelling evaluation task, in Section 8 we discuss our thoughts on the results, in Section 9 we announce the planned future experiments. Examples in this paper will be mostly given in K'iche', Chukchi and English. English examples, while English being neither an agglutinative or polysynthetic language, are given in

Proceedings of the first workshop on NLP applications to field linguistics, pages 77–85
July 5–10, 2020. ©2020 Association for Computational Linguistics
https://doi.org/10.26615/978-954-452-056-4_009

order for the reader to better understand the examples.

2 Languages

We perform the experiments using two languages: K'iche' (ISO-639: quc), a Mayan language of Guatemala that is of the agglutinating type, and Chukchi (ISO-639: ckt), a Chukotko-Kamchatkan language of Siberia of the polysynthetic type. Both of these types are characterised by words consisting of a large number of individual morphs, surface representations of morphemes.

The following examples in K'iche' (1) and Chukchi (2) demonstrate this tendency.[1]

(1) X-in-e'-ki-k'am-a'
CP-B1SG-MOV-A3PL-receive-DEP
'They went to take me'

Both languages exhibit polypersonal agreement (both the subject and object arguments of transitive verbs are encoded on the verb), and Chukchi, in addition, exhibits noun incorporation. As it can be seen in example 2, the object *манэ* /mane/ 'money' is incorporated, rendering intransitive the transitive root *ванłя* /wanła/ 'ask'.

(2) Нэмыӄэй ны-манэ-ванłя-сӄэв-ӄэна-т.
nemәqej nә-mane-wanła-sqew-qena-t
also ST-money-ask-MCP-ST.3SG-PL
'They also came to ask for money'

Languages of these types are widespread across the Americas but infrequent in Europe and, as a result, were less researched in terms of predictive text input.

2.1 Data

As K'iche' and Chukchi are low-resource languages, the availability of large corpora is limited. We use data annotated for morphological segments and unannotated text as well. For Chukchi, the annotated data comes from the ChukLang[2] corpus, we use a version that was extracted and converted to Cyrillic orthography to make it compatible with the unannotated corpus. The unannotated data comes from a collection of folklore and texts from the internet.

[1]Glossing symbols are from the original sources: CP 'completive', B1SG 'absolutive 1st person singular', MOV 'movement prefix', A3PL 'ergative 3rd person plural', DEP 'dependent status suffix, ST 'stative', MCP 'goal-oriented movement', ST.3SG '3rd person singular stative', PL 'plural'.

[2]https://chuklang.ru/

	Unannotated		Annotated	
	Sents	Words	Sents	Words
K'iche'	24,254	275,265	1,299	8,789
Chukchi	33,322	151,585	1,006	4,417

Table 1: Dataset sizes for the two languages measured in sentences and words. Unannotated and annotated datasets do not intersect. Annotation was done manually.

For K'iche' we also use annotated and unannotated texts. The annotated texts are a hand-segmented set of sentences used in constructing a morphologically and syntactically annotated corpus of K'iche', these sentences come from a range of sources including grammar-book and dictionary examples, stories and legal texts. This corpus is well described in Tyers and Henderson (2021).

The second, unannotated, portion of the data is obtained from the *An Crúbadán* project done by Scannell (2007), that collected corpora from the web for indigenous and marginalised languages.

Table 1 shows the amount of data available for both languages.

2.2 Preprocessing

In order to segment the raw data using a morphological segmentation model the annotated data is split into two disjoint subsets: train (50 percent) and test (50 percent). This ratio is chosen due to low annotated data volume – we suppose that a choice of a disbalanced ratio like 80 percent/20 percent can lead to unreliable results. The automatically segmented corpus is then used for language modelling, while the test split of annotated data is used for predictive text.

3 Related work

Being one of the latest works on language modelling of indigenous languages, Schwartz et al. (2020) proposed the usage of morphological segmentation in order to improve metrics of language modelling. The authors compared different segmentation methods, such as single words, dividing into characters, BPE, Morfessor, Finite-state transducers (FST). Unfortunately, the authors could not do the end-task evaluation of the trained models but suggested doing predictive text as evaluation.

Boudreau et al. (2020), devoted to Mi'kmaq language modelling evaluation, gave us ideas on how to approach the language modelling task. Mi'kmaq (ISO-639: `mic`), an Eastern Algonquian low-resourse polysynthetic language, is spoken primarily in Eastern Canada and has around 8700 speakers. Not only did the authors work with indigenous language, but they also did the keystroke savings evaluation, which is pretty similar to the predictive text evaluation described in the previous work.

There are other works – Suhartono. et al. (2014); Yu et al. (2017) – that described keystroke savings evaluation. What is more important, the authors worked with agglutinative languages, Bahasa (ISO-639, `ind`), the official language of Indonesia, and Korean (ISO-639, `kor`), official and national language of both North Korea and South Korea (originally Korea). Though we do not want to use the same language modelling technics as were described in the papers, we still find it inspiring there are works dedicated to this task.

As we mentioned before, we assume that the usage of morphs while doing text prediction will make it both effective and ergonomic; in the same time, morphological segmentation brings new challenges. Lane and Bird (2020), devoted to Kunwinjku, a polysynthetic language of northern Australia, and Turkish, showed that morph-based autocomplete for polysynthetic languages can be troublesome due to long words and sparse vocabularies of such languages. Moreover, dialectal variations and dealing with input errors using edit distance makes the next-morpheme predictioning even harder, so, as it is shown in the paper, Turkish may be a more attractive language for morph-based predictioning than Kunwinjku.

4 Tasks

As mentioned previously, our experiments are split into four distinct tasks, from the more fundamental to the more application-specific. In the following sections we describe the methodology for these tasks and the results obtained.

Segmentation We use several segmentation methods in order to compare morphological segmentation and statistical one.

Language modelling We do 10-fold cross-validation in order to train models for end-task evaluation. The evaluation metric is word and character level perplexity. Although the model we use allows both character and word level training, in this paper we do word level training with subwords serving as words.

Predictive text entry We take the trained models from the former task and compare their performance in the predictive text task. The task is to predict the next linguistic unit of output for a given input looking at the top-3 predictions. The evaluation measure is average number of clicks per character and keystroke savings rate. The fewer clicks per character the less the end-user has to type. It is important to mention that the first segment of each word is always typed character by character; this is caused by the model not having token `<bos>` (beginning of the sentence) in its design and the fact that we are doing word level training. As mentioned above, we use the cross-validation models for this task.

Significance testing As the main tasks – language modelling and predictive text – are done using cross-validation, we have sets of results for each model. These results are tested in order to say if some models are significantly better than the others. To do this, first, we do the one-way ANOVA[3] with the null hypothesis being "all the means are the same". In case the null hypothesis is rejected, we then do pairwise Least Significant Difference test (LSD-test)[4] to group the models so that we can find the best performing ones which are not significantly different from each other. The LSD values are given in the appendix.

5 Segmentation

The idea to compare statistical and morphological segmentation was already tested by other researchers; for example, Pan et al. (2020) showed that the usage of morphological segmentation significantly improves the BLEU and ChrF3 metrics in neural machine translation (NMT).

In this paper we want to compare statistical segmentation, presented by Unigram (Kudo, 2018) and WordPiece (Schuster and Nakajima, 2012), and morphological segmentation[5]. We choose NeuralMorphemeSegmentation (NMS; Sorokin and Kravtsova, 2018) for morphological segmentation

[3](2008) One-Way Analysis of Variance. In: The Concise Encyclopedia of Statistics. Springer, New York, NY. `https://doi.org/10.1007/978-0-387-32833-1_297`

[4](2008) Least Significant Difference Test. In: The Concise Encyclopedia of Statistics. Springer, New York, NY. `https://doi.org/10.1007/978-0-387-32833-1_226`

[5]We also tried BPE but as the results did not surpass the other systems we exclude them for matters of space and clarity of presentation.

Variant	Example
Input text	*Xke'x ri nukinaq'*
Canonical	x# ke'x$ ri nu# kinaq'$
NMS	x# ke'x$ ri nu# kinaq'$
Unigram	xke# '# x$ ri nuki# na# q'$
WordPiece	xk# e'x$ ri nuk# inaq'$

Table 2: Segmentation variants for the K'iche' sentence *Xke'x ri nukinaq'* "My beans were ground". The canonical segmentation corresponds to /CP-grind.PASS the POSS.1SG-bean/. The hash symbol, #, indicates that there is a segment after the current one and the dollar symbol, $, indicates the last segment in a multi-segment word.

as we have already used it before and it showed good results.

As an output format, as a base we use the stem with singular suffix strategy mentioned in Pan et al. (2020). We modify the strategy, so that all of the subwords are treated the same way: single-morpheme words remain unchanged, in composite words every morpheme except the last one ends with #, the last morpheme ends with $. Table 2 demonstrates the format.

6 Language modelling

Merity et al. (2017) proposed the usage of an AWD-LSTM model for language modelling, showing that it achieves state-of-the-art word level perplexities on Penn treebank and WikiText-2. This model was applied in Schwartz et al. (2020) to several indigenous languages, including Chukchi, and showed good performance. The model trains fast, allows to be trained both on character level and word level, and also is good dealing with overfitting, which is essential while working with low-resource languages.

Although BERT (Devlin et al., 2019) has been successfully used for low-resource languages, Ngoc Le and Sadat (2020) and Wang et al. (2020) showed that models based on BERT models usually have hundreds of millions of parameters and as such are not efficient enough in terms of space for existing mobile phones. This is not suitable for us as our main goal is to use the model for a phone keyboard in order to do predictive text. For all the mentioned reasons we use the described above AWD-LSTM as our model.

The data for language modelling is at first split into modelling (80 percent) and test (20 percent) subsets. Then for the 10-fold cross-validation the modelling subset is split into train (75 percent) and validation (25 percent) subsets. The folds are made using ShuffleSplit[6] with the same seed as the one used while language modelling. The dictionaries for the embeddings consist of all the subwords of train dataset plus the `<unk>` token; the validation subset is used to calculate perplexity in the end of each epoch. The models are trained until 5 epochs without perplexity improvement on a validation subset.

The training hyperparameters are included in the appendix.

6.1 Modelling type

All the models we train can be divided into three types: single-way segmented, two-way segmented and finetuned models.

In order to distinguish a language model from a segmentation method the model names will be given in **bold** e.g. Unigram is a segmentation model while **Unigram** is a model trained on data processed by the corresponding segmentation model.

6.1.1 Single-way segmented

Models of this type – **NMS**, **Unigram**, **Wordpiece** – are trained using datasets from Section 5.

6.1.2 Two-way segmented

Models of this type – **NMS+Unigram**, **NMS+Wordpiece** – are trained using two datasets from Section 5 concatenated together. The idea behind this modelling type is that we want to see if having data processed by different segmentation methods can help us solve both tasks on a high level.

6.1.3 Finetuning

As it was proposed in one of the related works (Boudreau et al., 2020), pretrained embeddings can be used in order to improve the performance of the language models. We check if finetuning will allow us to get better scores both for language modelling and predictive text.

Models of this type – **Unigram2NMS**, **Wordpiece2NMS** – are at first trained using the Unigram/Wordpiece data and then we use morphologically segmented data to finetune the model. Looking ahead we should also mention that it turned out there is no need to lower the learning rate of the

[6]`https://scikit-learn.org/0.24/modules/generated/sklearn.model_selection.ShuffleSplit.html`

model while finetuning it as it only lengthens the training.

It is worth mentioning that not only embeddings, but also RNN layers are being pretrained.

6.2 Results

All the results are tested as described in Section 4, Significance testing and as we can see in Table 3, the best models for K'iche' and Chukchi according to perplexity are **NMS** and finetuning models.

	K'iche'		Chukchi	
	Wd	Ch	Wd	Ch
NMS	**32.59**	**7.57**	**176.56**	**27.04**
Uni	35.29	8.20	464.43	71.13
WP	148.24	34.45	2745.33	420.48
Uni2NMS	34.32	7.97	**163.58**	**25.05**
WP2NMS	**32.06**	**7.45**	**165.90**	**25.41**
NMS+Uni	34.10	7.92	265.67	40.71
NMS+WP	54.27	12.61	524.28	80.34

Table 3: Word (Wd) level and character (Ch) level perplexities for the models (mean scores of 10-fold cross-validation). **NMS** stands for **NeuralMorphemeSegmentation**, **Uni** stands for **Unigram**, **WP** stands for **Wordpiece**. We do not give subword level perplexities as they are not comparable. The best scores are in **bold** being significantly better according to ANOVA than the others but not outperforming each other.

The two-way segmented models show lower scores than **NMS** ones, though they are better than the models trained on data of their statistical origin (Unigram, Wordpiece segmenters). It does seem like the usage of morphologically segmentated data allows us to improve the performance of the models.

It is worth saying that perplexity scores for different segmentations can not be compared to each other as is due to the dictionary sizes of all the models being different. In order to do so we need to use not subword, but word and character perplexity. Mielke (2019) describes a method of computing them from subword perplexity, so we decide to use the given formulae.

The normalization of scores is done in a following way: at first, the negative log-likelihood of the strings is computed:

$$\text{nll} = \log \text{ppl}^{\text{sw}} * (C_{\text{sw}} + k) \quad (1)$$

where nll is negative log-likehood, ppl^{sw} is the computed subword level perplexity, C_{sw} is the total count of subwords in the set and k is the total count of lines in the set that stands for the count of `<eos>` tokens, which are also predicted by the model.

Then word level and character level perplexities are calculated using the negative log-likehood we get on a previous step:

$$\text{ppl}^{w} = \exp \frac{\text{nll}}{C_w + k} \quad (2)$$

$$\text{ppl}^{c} = \exp \frac{\text{nll}}{C_c + k} \quad (3)$$

where ppl^{w} is word level perplexity, ppl^{c} is character level perplexity, nll is negative log-likehood, C_w is the total count of words in the set, C_c is the total count of characters in the set and k is the total count of lines in the set.

7 Predictive text input

In order to evaluate the models we do predictive text input. The idea is that we automatically emulate a person using a smart keyboard while it is offering some predictions, which have to be meaningful. The meaningfulness is important because we assume that the typing person would like to choose from real words/morphs and not some artificial subwords that make at best no sense and in a worst case scenario they may mean something totally wrong (3). The example is given in Turkish because it illustrates the problem well.

(3) a. araba-m-a
car-POSS.1SG-DAT
'into my car'

b. arab-am-a
arab-*vulgar.word*-DAT
'arab into *vulgar word*'

While evaluating, we look through top 3 model predictions and compare them to the subword we are currently predicting. If they are equal, that prediction is chosen, otherwise we look at the next one. If none of the predictions were correct, we consider that the user will have to finish the word character by character. Thus, a total number of clicks for a word is computed to measure clicks per character metric:

$$\text{CpC} = \frac{\text{keys}_{\text{prediction}}}{\text{keys}_{\text{normal}}} \quad (4)$$

,

where CpC is clicks per character, $\text{keys}_{\text{prediction}}$ is the count of predicted clicks (spaces are included),

$\text{keys}_{\text{normal}}$ is the count of clicks needed to input the word character by character.

We also include the keystroke savings rate used in Boudreau et al. (2020) so that we can compare our results with theirs:

$$KSR = \frac{\text{keys}_{\text{normal}} - \text{keys}_{\text{prediction}}}{\text{keys}_{\text{normal}}} * 100 \quad (5)$$

, where KSR stands for keystroke savings rate.

7.1 Results

All the results are tested as described in Section 4, Significance testing and as we can see in Table 4, for K'iche' the best model is **NMS+Wordpiece** and for Chuckhi the best ones are **NMS**, **Wordpiece2NMS** and **NMS+Unigram** – the same group is second best for K'iche'.

Predictive text metrics do correlate with language-modelling metrics; even though **NMS+Wordpiece** performs the best for K'iche', the group of **NMS** and **Wordpiece2NMS** has both best perplexity and clicks per character scores. We suppose that the models that use morphologically segmented data perform better in this task because the used evaluation data, while not being used in language modelling, resembles the training data, as both these sets are morph-based.

The results for Chukchi are worse than the results for K'iche'. The reason may be that gold standard for Chukchi is in Telqep Chukchi, while the corpus used for training is in standard Chukchi. Another reason may be that words in K'iche' evaluation data are shorter both segmentwise and characterwise than the Chukchi words, as shown in Table 5. In case a model can not predict a correct morph, we penalise it by making the whole word be typed character-by-character, so the longer the word is, the more significant mistakes become.

8 Discussion

As we can see, the evaluation shows that there is no single model that outperforms the others in both languages, but models that use morphologically segmented data generally show higher scores. Thus we recommend to try morphological segmentation as it can be used with a statistical one. It is important to mention is that there is no need in training models using morphologically segmented data from scratch, the existing models can be finetuned and the results will not differ significantly from the ones of **NMS**.

	K'iche'		**Chukchi**	
	CpC	KSR	CpC	KSR
No prediction	1.00	0.00	1.00	0.00
NMS	0.96	3.03	**0.99**	**0.78**
Unigram	0.98	1.46	0.99	0.26
Wordpiece	0.97	2.35	0.99	0.20
Unigram2NMS	0.96	3.49	0.99	0.69
Wordpiece2NMS	0.96	3.53	**0.99**	**0.79**
NMS+Unigram	0.96	3.53	**0.99**	**0.73**
NMS+Wordpiece	**0.95**	**4.26**	0.99	0.68

Table 4: Predictive keyboard metrics, the number of clicks per character (CpC) and keystroke savings rate (KSR) for each of the methods. 'No prediction' means that the user has to input all the words character by character including spaces, serving as baseline. The best scores are in **bold** being significantly better according to ANOVA than the others but not than each other.

	SpW	**CpW**
Chukchi	2.54	8.83
K'iche'	1.56	5.20

Table 5: Segments per word (SpW) and characters per word (CpW) metrics of the evaluation datasets.

K'iche' models in all the tasks have better performance than Chukchi models. While we do not know the particular reason for this, we assume that the polysynthetic language complexity may be hindering the model from training. In the mentioned above Lane and Bird (2020) the authors also reported that polysynthetic languages have their special challenges such as high word length, complexity, etc.

As we reference Boudreau et al. (2020), it seems reasonable to compare the results of their experiments with the results of ours. As our task was to predict *linguistic* units, not any kind of units, while in the Mi'kmaq paper words and BPE segments were being predicted, comparison of the results may seem not really correct; though if we do compare the results, we can see that the best KSR score for Mi'kmaq is **3.81**, while the best score for K'iche' is **4.26**. At the same time, the best Chukchi KSR (**0.79**) is much worse that the Mi'kmaq score.

Alongside the metrics we compute there is also a metric which requires end-user testing – the sanity check. As mentioned before, the issue with statistical segmentation is that subwords predicted and offered to the user may have no sense for the user or, what is much worse, may carry the wrong meaning. We do suppose that this alone can be a reason to choose morphological segmentation over the regular one because segmentation task is not done just for itself – it serves a purpose in a larger scheme of things. We think that in case the language model will be used in predictive text setting, where the user experience and user reaction is highly relevant, morphological segmentation should be chosen as a subword tokenisation method, while statistical segmentation may be chosen for machine translation, for example.

9 Future work

We plan to test several other language models and language modelling metrics in order to find out what correlates best with text prediction scores.

We find it reasonable to experiment on other languages, for example, Nahuatl and Yupik, in order to get a better understanding when the use of morphological segmentation is reasonable.

Another task to do is to run an end-user evaluation of multiple segmentations and determine which units are preferred. In order to do this, we also need to solve the problem of predictive text evaluation that the user has to input the first word character by character – to do this, we will possibly have to combine word level and character level based models.

Acknowledgements

We thank Robert Pugh for his comments and suggestions on an earlier version of this manuscript.

References

Jeremie Boudreau, Akankshya Patra, Ashima Suvarna, and Paul Cook. 2020. Evaluating the impact of subword information and cross-lingual word embeddings on mi'kmaq language modelling. In *Proceedings of the 12th Language Resources and Evaluation Conference*, pages 2736–2745, Marseille, France. European Language Resources Association.

Jacob Devlin, Ming-Wei Chang, Kenton Lee, and Kristina Toutanova. 2019. Bert: Pre-training of deep bidirectional transformers for language understanding.

Philip Gage. 1994. A new algorithm for data compression. *C Users J.*, 12(2):23–38.

Taku Kudo. 2018. Subword regularization: Improving neural network translation models with multiple subword candidates.

William Lane and Steven Bird. 2020. Interactive word completion for morphologically complex languages. In *Proceedings of the 28th International Conference on Computational Linguistics*, pages 4600–4611, Barcelona, Spain (Online). International Committee on Computational Linguistics.

Stephen Merity, Nitish Shirish Keskar, and Richard Socher. 2017. Regularizing and Optimizing LSTM Language Models. *arXiv preprint arXiv:1708.02182*.

Sabrina J. Mielke. 2019. Can you compare perplexity across different segmentations?

Tan Ngoc Le and Fatiha Sadat. 2020. Revitalization of indigenous languages through pre-processing and neural machine translation: The case of Inuktitut. In *Proceedings of the 28th International Conference on Computational Linguistics*, pages 4661–4666, Barcelona, Spain (Online). International Committee on Computational Linguistics.

Yirong Pan, Xiao Li, Yating Yang, and Rui Dong. 2020. Morphological word segmentation on agglutinative languages for neural machine translation.

Kevin Scannell. 2007. The Crúbadán Project: Corpus building for under-resourced languages. In *Proceedings of the 3rd Web as Corpus Workshop*, pages 5–15.

Mike Schuster and Kaisuke Nakajima. 2012. Japanese and korean voice search. In *International Conference on Acoustics, Speech and Signal Processing*, pages 5149–5152.

Lane Schwartz, Francis Tyers, Lori Levin, Christo Kirov, Patrick Littell, Chi kiu Lo, Emily Prud'hommeaux, Hyunji Hayley Park, Kenneth Steimel, Rebecca Knowles, Jeffrey Micher, Lonny Strunk, Han Liu, Coleman Haley, Katherine J. Zhang, Robbie Jimmerson, Vasilisa Andriyanets, Aldrian Obaja Muis, Naoki Otani, Jong Hyuk Park, and Zhisong Zhang. 2020. Neural polysynthetic language modelling.

Alexey Sorokin and Anastasia Kravtsova. 2018. Deep convolutional networks for supervised morpheme segmentation of russian language. In *Artificial Intelligence and Natural Language*, pages 3–10, Cham. Springer International Publishing.

Derwin Suhartono., Garry Wong., Polim Kusuma., and Silviana Saputra. 2014. Predictive text system for bahasa with frequency, n-gram, probability table and syntactic using grammar. In *Proceedings of the 6th International Conference on Agents and Artificial Intelligence - Volume 1: ICAART,*, pages 305–311. INSTICC, SciTePress.

Francis Tyers and Robert Henderson. 2021. A corpus of K'iche' annotated for morphosyntactic structure. In *Proceedings of the First Workshop on Natural Language Processing for Indigenous Languages of the Americas*, pages 10–20, Online. Association for Computational Linguistics.

Zihan Wang, Karthikeyan K, Stephen Mayhew, and Dan Roth. 2020. Extending multilingual bert to low-resource languages.

Seunghak Yu, Nilesh Kulkarni, Haejun Lee, and Jihie Kim. 2017. Syllable-level neural language model for agglutinative language.

A Hyperparameters

Here we provide hyperparameter values for the various models to aid in reproduction of the results.

A.1 Morphological segmentation

In this section we describe the best hyperparameter settings that we found for the various tasks.

A.1.1 NeuralMorphemeSegmentation

The best results for morphological segmentation are achieved with this hyperparameters:

Parameter	K'iche'	Chuckhi
convolutional layers	3	3
window size	3 – 4	4–6
filters	96	96
dense output users	64	20
context dropout	0.3	0.3
memorize morphemes	no	no
memorize ngram counts.	no	no

Table 6: NMS hyperparameters.

A.2 Least Significant Deviation values

The LSD-test results for language modelling and predictive text tasks (this value is used to arrange the tasks results into groups where all the values have no significant difference):

Task	K'iche'	Chukchi
language modelling	1.494	17.806
predictive text	14.22e-4	6.779e-4

Table 7: LSD values

A.3 Language modelling

All the models based on Merity et al. (2017) are trained with the hyperparameters in Table 8.

Parameter	Value
LSTM layers	3
embedding dim	256
hidden units per layer	3000
use regularization	no
layers dropout	0.4
RNN layers dropout	0.1
embeddings dropout	0.1
remove words from embeddings dropout	0.0
sequence length	100
optimizer	Adam
learning rate	1e-3
weight decay	1.2e-6
seed	1111

Table 8: AWD-LSTM hyperparameters.

B Evaluation

System	Sentence
Raw	*ri tapa'l kub'an k'ax we man ch'ajom taj*
Gloss	'When the *nance*[1] is not washed, it can cause a lot of damage.'
NMS	r i _ t a p a ' l _ k u **b'an** _ **k'ax** _ w e _ m a n _ c h ' a j o m _ **taj** _
Unigram	r i _ t a p a ' l _ k u b ' a n _ k ' a x _ w e _ m a n _ c h ' a j o m _ **taj** _
Wordpiece	r i _ t a p a ' l _ k u b ' a n _ k ' a x _ w e _ **man** _ c h ' a j o m _ **taj** _
Raw	*jawi xkib'ij wi chi ke'e wi*
Gloss	'Where did they say that they would go?'
NMS	j a w i _ x **ki b'ij** _ **wi** _ **chi** _ k e ' e _ w i _
Unigram	j a w i _ x k i b ' i j _ w i _ c h i _ k e ' e _ w i _
Wordpiece	j a w i _ x k i b ' i j _ w i _ c h i _ k e ' e _ w i _
Raw	*kamik kewa' pa taq ri b'e*
Gloss	'Today they will eat on the way.'
NMS	k a m i k _ k e w a ' _ **pa** _ **taq** _ **ri** _ b ' e _
Unigram	k a m i k _ k e w a ' _ p a _ t a q _ **ri** _ b ' e _
Wordpiece	k a m i k _ k e w a ' _ p a _ **taq** _ r i _ **b'e** _

Table 9: Examples of text prediction by single-way segmented models for K'iche' (see Section 6). Underscores indicate word boundaries. Segments in **bold** were correct morph or word guesses. [1] *Byrsonima crassifolia*, a species of flowering plant.

Author Index

Association for Computational Linguistics
209 N. Eighth Street
Stroudsburg, Pennsylvania 18360

ISBN 978-1-7138-6151-5

CURRAN ASSOCIATES INC.
proceedings.com